CARE AND BEHAVIOUR OF THE
German Shepherd Dog

CARE AND BEHAVIOUR OF THE
German Shepherd Dog

DR DAVID SANDS

The Crowood Press

First published in 2004 by
The Crowood Press Ltd
Ramsbury, Marlborough
Wiltshire SN8 2HR

www.crowood.com

British Library Cataloguing-in-Publication Data
A catalogue record for this book is available from the British Library.

ISBN 1 86126 713 4

Dedication
To my son, Maximillian Alexander Sands

Photography by the author, Dr David Sands.

Enquiries to the author should be directed to drdavidsands@aol.com

Edited and designed by OutHouse Publishing Services,
Shalbourne, Marlborough, Wiltshire SN8 3QJ

Printed and bound in Singapore by Craft Print International

Contents

Acknowledgements   6

Introduction   7

   1   A Brief Breed History   11

   2   Breed Personality   15

   3   Becoming a German Shepherd Dog Owner   21

   4   Training   43

   5   Re-homing a German Shepherd   65

   6   Problem Behaviour   81

   7   Health   107

Conclusion   127

Index   128

Acknowledgements

I should like to thank especially those people who directly helped in the research, photography and production of this book: my wife, Catherine, who is genuinely 'dog phobic' and yet gave me continued support; Max, my youngest son, who enjoys being a 'model' around the best German Shepherd Dogs; and Lancashire police dog handlers PC John Birkett and PC Gareth Dixon with their dogs Hobbs and Nelson. I would also thank the Pet Care Trust breeders' directory, and the fate that led me to a wonderful GSD breeder, Marian Marsden and her daughters Carol Marsden and Judith Gratton. This closely knit local family, spread across three homes, own a splendid group of dogs, all of them kept in their respective homes as companion pets. These dogs, Remy, Bess, Cassie, Laddie, Poppi and Megan are a credit to the family's love and affection for the breed. Nothing was too much trouble for Marian, Carol and Judith (and her children, Ruth and Daniel) when I needed to take the many pictures to illustrate this book. They helped to make my year-long photography project a pleasure rather than a task.

I took great pleasure in watching Carol lovingly support Remy as she gave birth to the 'Magnificent Seven' (with Caesarean complications). I also observed Carol's dedication as she expertly cared for the puppies as they were weaned in the seven weeks before they left to go to new homes. The family eagerly read through an early draft of this book and made useful comments. I hope that our friendship will continue beyond this book and long into the future. The breed is in extremely safe hands if others care for their dogs as this family clearly does.

I should also like to take this opportunity to sincerely thank my many clients who, indirectly, gave me the important clinical experience that enabled me to understand the German Shepherd's many attributes and man-made flaws. I was certainly naïve when I first began in practice in 1995 with the kind help of the leading animal behaviourist, Dr Peter Neville. Veterinary surgeons Michael Clarke, Christopher Lord, Sue Shuttleworth and Christopher Manning have supported me from these early days. My continuing research into canine anal-gland disorders and the potential link to behavioural disorders has been helped by discussion with, and referrals made by, these distinguished practitioners.

Finally, thanks to my editor Elizabeth Mallard-Shaw for bringing structure to the thousands of words, and to all at Crowood Press. Here's to the book being long in print!

Introduction

The German Shepherd Dog is one of the most distinctive breeds known today, and – not surprisingly to GSD lovers – it has retained 'top-breed' status for most of the 20th century. It is a powerful dog that can bring down the toughest criminal, protect the smallest child, and follow the most complicated instructions that handlers wish to give to it. It is also a breed that in the wrong hands can become a social menace capable of inflicting fatal wounds on an unsuspecting human or other dog. It is the archetypal 'wolf in our living rooms'.

Born to Work

Most of today's German Shepherds are kept not as working dogs but as companion animals. Nevertheless, some knowledge of the working background of the German Shepherd is absolutely critical if the breed's behavioural traits are to be understood. Analysis of its origins, especially as a guarding dog, explains the desirable facets of its personality – faithfulness and obedience – as well as the aggressive traits that are not always desirable.

There is a working role for the breed today, but its 'shepherd' name tag somewhat belies that niche. Its active role lies not in livestock herding – that is a job for the Border Collie – but in guarding, for which purpose it has long been championed by the armed forces, the police, customs officers, and the prison service. Most security companies commissioned to patrol property also make full use of the innate guarding instincts of the German Shepherd. All the uniformed services seek out the individual with the dominant, fearless and 'controllable aggressive' tendencies and will promote these characteristics in the animal's working tasks. Aggression on demand is required, so predatory, protective, possessive and territorial traits can be observed as desirable when placed in this context. In a companion animal, on the other hand, such behaviours can bring a dog and his owner into disrepute.

It is important to realize that the companion dog and the working animal are not fundamentally different: the companion-dog version of the breed has all the intelligence, instinct and alertness of the working dog. However, appropriate training from an early stage can determine how these characteristics are expressed. For the companion dog, the expression of the guarding behaviours is suppressed: such a dog would never display aggression towards anyone – family members, strangers and other dogs alike.

The trained companion dog recalls at once to the sound of his or her name or to the sound of a dog whistle and will calmly walk by an owner's side through the busiest street thoroughfare. An owner of such a well-trained and happy German Shepherd is rightly proud of such a companion. Properly socialized and carefully trained, the German Shepherd can be a family's best friend.

In sharp contrast to this properly trained companion dog, a German Shepherd that has experienced a troubled early life and no socialization (at the litter stage and beyond) will have a poor temperament. He will be difficult to control and difficult to live with – for everyone, not just his owner. Such a dog can only lead people to demonize the breed (although this also applies to a great number of other strong and powerful breeds, especially those that have been selected for fighting traits).

The strong-willed, guarding dog in the breed will always revert to instinct when of a nervous disposition. The dog that has been poorly or inadequately socialized (those that are a result of accidental matings, puppy farms, mixed breed commercial kennels) will display uncontrolled possessive, protective, predatory, territorial and fear aggression, and many other nervous behaviours. The nervous German Shepherd will direct aggression towards moving targets, other dogs, strangers, and even family members. It is in these circumstances that the media and the anti-dog circle often refer to the German Shepherd as the 'Alsatian' dog – the term first coined as a

This keen-eyed German Shepherd Dog, encountered by the author during filming for the BBC's 999 series, had been trained for HM Prison Service. Many people are attracted to the intelligence and working instincts of the breed, but they require a calm companion animal, not a working dog.

result of anti-German feeling after the First World War and now deemed derogatory.

The Domesticated 'Wolf'

When showing unprovoked and uncontrolled aggression, a German Shepherd fits most people's stereotype of the wolf. All the domesticated dogs that have been tested to date reveal that they share an amount of wolf DNA. This fact doesn't necessarily mean that the domesticated dog came directly from the wolf but rather that they share a common ancestor with other canines such as the jackal. The European Grey, or 'Timber', wolf might well be an evolutionary close cousin of the German Shepherd. Even if it isn't, the physical resemblance is enough for most people to make comparisons. I have a dog-phobic relative who believes that all dogs are killers regardless of their appearance and disposition, but she believes the GSD is the worst. I am fairly sure you won't be surprised to know that she was bitten, both as a child and as a teenager, by a German Shepherd Dog

All inherited or innate behaviour shown by our domesticated breeds is to some extent paralleled in lupine behaviour. Circling, rounding up, mesmerizing with the eye, and crawling, are basic hunting behaviours. Guarding instinct comes from wanting to 'protect' the pack, defend the 'kill', and see off competitors and rivals. In other words, behind those keen eyes, and beneath those erect ears and distinctive, proudly held head and sloping stance of the alert, healthy German Shepherd, is an animal not so distinct from a tamed wolf.

However, the negative attention that the GSD has somewhat unfairly attracted over the past decades would baffle any self-respecting wolf, who would undoubtedly disown the image of the demon that is so often portrayed in the media. Nevertheless, such

attention compounds the problem for the GSD: attacks on children or vulnerable people and the sheer numbers of German Shepherds and GSD crossbreeds in rescue centres does nothing to promote the breed to those families seeking a faithful yet strong, gentle and good-natured companion dog.

The nasty reputation of antisocial German Shepherds has, in recent decades, been transferred to Rottweilers, Dobermans and Pit Bull Terriers. And it is true, the 'wolf in the dog' can cause horrendous problems, but it is important to realize that this is not just the fault of the dogs. Neither is it always just the fault of the owner, whatever the late Barbara Woodhouse's assertion, 'There's no such thing as a bad dog, just bad owners!' A range of factors combine to influence the

When showing unprovoked aggression, the German Shepherd probably represents most people's stereotype of the wolf.

temperament and behaviour of a dog, and inadequate socialization from the litter stage onwards is one of the most important of these. When an inexperienced, unsuspecting owner acquires a nervous puppy that has been poorly socialized, or perhaps even abused, problems develop very quickly. Even the best-intentioned and motivated owner can struggle with a neurotic 'wolf in companion dog's clothing'.

A New Perspective

Such problems are compounded when an owner makes the common mistake of confusing loyalty and faithfulness with insecurity. A faithful companion animal is not the same as a canine shadow that has lost his ability to be independent and secure. It is folly to foster the latter traits in any dog, but in a German Shepherd it can result in disaster. They can become extremely possessive over owners to the degree that other humans and dogs have to be 'chased off' because they represent competition for affection or simply a thing to fear.

In the early stages of hyper-attachment, an enthusiastic, over-dependent dog will massage the owner's ego. It's wonderful to be 'loved' in what appears to be such an unconditional way and always to be greeted with an enthusiasm that proves the dog cannot bear to be separate from you. However, there is no such thing as unconditional love. Dogs have their own agendas, and these can be analysed by animal behaviourists. A dog whose agenda is not fully understood can become frustrated, neurotic, aggressive, insecure, withdrawn and, worst of all, so misguided that tragedy can result.

My aim in this book is to encourage the reader to switch perspectives: to try to see the world through a German Shepherd's eyes. It is then that informed training can begin. It is then that the relationship between companion dog and owner can be correctly established and highly rewarding. It is no use projecting human intelligence and understanding of the world onto a German Shepherd Dog. He simply doesn't see things our way. All too commonly, instinct is mistaken for intelligence. A dog does not possess the frontal lobes of our brain. For the dog there is an instinctive capacity to recall scents, trails and territory and to recognize the schedules that define daily life in the human-canine pack. But there is no clearly defined yesterday, today and tomorrow: there is 'now'. There is understanding by association – the ability to associate sounds or actions with consequent actions or particular events; but dogs do not understand the human language in either written or spoken form. It is all gobbledegook to them.

This book will examine the importance of communication, socialization, instinctive pack behaviour and learned behaviour. It will explore the relationship between humans and companion dogs. In addition it will give practical guidance on how to select a happy puppy; how to successfully rescue an adult dog; how to train and how to guide a dog *psychologically* rather than physically. There is also advice on the important aspects of the day-to-day practical care of a puppy, semi-adult and a mature dog. Throughout, the book aims to help you to understand your German Shepherd Dog. Just as importantly, perhaps, it shows you how to help your German Shepherd Dog understand you!

1   A Brief Breed History

The German Shepherd Dog originates from a period in 19th-century Europe when many domesticated breeds were being selectively bred for size, shape, colour and behavioural characteristics that would fit them for a specific working task. The German Shepherd was soon acknowledged to be perfectly suited for livestock and property guarding.

Once breeding stocks were exported and established across Europe and America, this physically distinctive, intelligent canine developed into a popular companion and guard dog. The popular German Shepherd we know so well has certainly undergone a number of physical changes over the past centuries. There have been many deliberate changes or selected variations in the ears, tail, coat thickness, colour and overall body shape over the decades. Even in this new millennium some distinctive variations can be seen in the German Shepherd. They provide a clue to the types developed by 18th- and 19th-century farmers in Germany and bordering countries.

Highland and Lowland Dogs

Historical references suggest that two primary types of dog, from a wide range of size, shape and colour, gave rise to the German Shepherd that exists today.

A highland dog, which was later to become known as the 'Thuringian type', was em-ployed exclusively as a working breed alongside livestock in rural farming communities. These dogs were said to be medium-sized, strongly built, and mostly uniform grey, with upright ears, and often with a small curled tail. In contrast, another distinctive form was identified and later became known as the Wurttemburg type. This German Shepherd type was also a herding dog but could be distinguished from the former by its much stockier body, bushy tail, and coat colour variations from tan and brown to grey and black.

Across Europe, where countries are not separated by water or mountain barriers,

Alongside all other breeds of domestic dog, the German Shepherd shares a common ancestor with jackals and wolves.

there were certainly many inbetween variations derived from these two basic types. However, selective breeding by farmers, which had helped to produce working dogs, meant the two types were ideally suited to the primary working tasks set for them. The rural people of middle and western Europe desired a range of specific characteristics to suit herding, livestock control and guarding. The farmers also wanted a mentally and physically strong dog that could work instinctively and yet also respond to basic signals from his master.

Established Breed Standards

Between the 1880s and 1890s a German Shepherd Dog breed standard, incorporating the two contrasting types, was established in Germany with the formation of the Verein für Deutsche Schäferhunde (German Shepherd Dog Association) later referred to and known as SV. Credit for its foundation in 1899 and the development of breed standards is given to ex-military man Max von Stephanitz. His 'highland style' dog, known as a Thuringian type, was the first to be registered in the breed club. From a rather humble beginning, with merely a handful of members at the turn of the 20th century, there were soon to be thousands of members in the years preceding the outbreak of the First World War.

Perhaps, rather understandably, the winners of these early breed shows significantly influenced the German Shepherd types that we see today. The two distinctive Thuringian and Wurttemburg types subsequently became the most successful stud-dogs and breeding bitches. These dogs displayed an excellent striding gait, combined with swiftness and alertness, characteristics that enabled them to win at the breed club shows of the time. An all-black form was a frequent show winner in Germany and Austria in these early

years of breed development and so became extremely popular at stud.

I have deliberately chosen not to dwell on the finer detailed history of the breed because such information will not particularly help a current owner train or deal with unwanted behaviours in his or her GSD. There are a number of books that offer this kind of information, and it is not necessary to become bogged down here with the names of the many famous sires and dams.

However, Max von Stephanitz should, quite rightly, be credited not only with establishing the first successful breed club for the German Shepherd, the German Shepherd Dog Association, but also for creating various forms of psychological and physiological assessments for the breed. A great percentage of his original measures are still used today. He wanted to maintain the working, protective and obedient skills of the breed.

The outbreak of the world wars meant that anything with the name 'German' in the title had a negative association. Thus the primary breed name, German Shepherd, was supplanted by the secondary name, Alsatian, and both names are in use today. There is a common misconception that the Alsatian is the smooth-coated variety of the breed and that the German Shepherd is the long-coated type. This is fallacious. The name Alsatian alludes to the French region of Alsace, and is in no way connected to type.

Breed Purity

The offspring of the show-winning dogs and bitches from the turn of the 20th century were soon to be exported across Europe and into the USA and Canada during the pre-war years. It is said and written that outside Germany, indiscriminate or non-selective breeding and cross-breeding produced inferior dogs with poor temperament and wildly contrasting shapes and colour forms. These dogs ranged from all white to pure black and all the potential colours in between. But then I suppose the purists would always argue that dilution of the breed and non-breed-standard dogs would be produced outside of Germany. I am not altogether convinced of this suggestion in that even with the supposedly high standards of modern-day breeding, the breed can still display undesirable traits.

The Kennel Club breed standard description for the German Shepherd Dog suggests that the breed should be: 'Steady of nerve, loyal, self-assured, courageous and tractable. Never nervous, over-aggressive or shy.' This rather idealized guide to temperament and its subjective descriptive terms would, I suspect, rule out a significant percentage of the dogs

being bred and shown in the UK and other countries today. Perhaps that is because it is the physical characteristics, rather than personality traits, that dominate the thoughts of most pedigree German Shepherd breeders.

There has been much discussion in the UK between GSD breeders about a need to 'go back' to what is supposed to be genetically stronger German stock. It has been said that UK (and perhaps also USA) stock is too interbred, and that there have been too many physical and psychological faults in the breed. For a number of years this has also been said of several popular breeds such as Boxers, Cocker and Springer Spaniels, and Labradors; and the importance of seeking out genes from other countries has been a commonly debated topic in dog circles.

The pure white colour form of the German Shepherd is considered to be a throwback to older breed lines. White German Shepherds cannot be entered in championship dog shows because they do not conform to the Kennel Club breed standard.

There are other dog breeders who say the same for Bulldogs and Mastiffs and countless other breeds.

It is certainly true that a small gene pool serves to concentrate and amplify any physical and psychological defects a particular breed may have. For example, in German Shepherds of the 1970s and beyond, the massive problem of hip dysplasia saw a strong breed reduced to an animal that could barely hold the powerful stance that is so visually striking in a healthy dog. It goes without saying that outside breeding stock brings in new genes. However, Teutonic German Shepherd Dog stock may well possess its own flaws, as I discovered from a local family who have successfully bred German Shepherds for many years. They purchased a German dog and found numerous problems that made him unsuitable as breeding stock.

The influence of German stock with its associated strong personality may create a more dominant dog in the UK that, while physically healthy, is more difficult for non-trainers to socialize and control. Too often, we are persuaded that the grass is greener on the other side, but I am fairly sure that American and German breeders have experienced just as many physical and psychological problems as have the UK breeders. However, outside of the UK, some authorities have introduced temperament tests that antisocial dogs have to undergo if their owners are to be allowed to keep them.

Three main hereditary physiological problems have beset the German Shepherd Dog for many decades and they continue to do so to a lesser extent to this present day. The first and most common defect, hip dysplasia, is a degenerative condition of the hip joint, which affects a dog's gait and causes poor mobility or lameness in the hind legs. Hip dysplasia is not exclusive to the GSD, but there has long been a breed predisposition, evidenced by veterinary records. The second defect, osteochondritis dissicans (OCD), affects joint cartilage in young dogs and, especially when combined with hip dysplasia, dramatically reduces the dog's ability to exercise. The third defect, progressive retinal atrophy, or PRA for short, leads to blindness in dogs.

Any of these defects, or a combination of them, adversely affects a dog's behaviour. Any condition that affects health and mobility will cause changes in temperament. We humans can be grumpy enough when we are suffering the effects of rheumatism or other aches and pains, and animals are no different in that respect. A 'happy dog' is healthy, and the offspring of such parent dogs will also be healthy with good temperament.

Most pedigree German Shepherd Dog breeding stock has now been cleared of these defects. However, some non-pedigree or crossbreed GSD-type dogs may still display and suffer from the effects of poor breeding. Ask the breeder for proof that the litter mother has undergone veterinary assessment for these defects and been cleared. If possible, immediately have a puppy fully screened and checked by your chosen veterinary surgeon because a professional breeder has responsibilities both in law and to the Kennel Club to provide a healthy puppy.

2 Breed Personality

The Working Dog

There are strong physical and mental characteristics in the German Shepherd that should always be taken into account when taking on the breed either as a puppy or as a re-homed dog. The adult GSD, apart from being used historically for livestock control (rather than herding), has been more actively employed by a great many organizations for both its guarding and protective instincts. In some fields, such as the military, they have been enthusiastically used for over 100 years in preference to similar breeds.

The German Shepherd is successfully utilized not only by the armed forces, but by the police, the prison service and security firms. All these organizations are looking for specific attributes in this breed. They require a dog that will bond with a handler; a dog that has the basic intelligence to be trained to take instruction that will help them instantly distinguish between friend and foe; a dog that can protect property and territory from intruders. These organizations want a working dog that learns quickly and can undertake a series of tasks correctly. They often need a powerful predator that can attack an identified target on command. The German Shepherd has the personality or instinctive traits to achieve all these tasks and, when correctly trained and employed in Schutzhund, he can perform them with ease.

(Schutzhund is protection work as defined in Europe. In Schutzhund trials, the dog is tested for his ability in tracking, agility and 'man work' – apprehension of a 'criminal').

The German Shepherd has been used in ways other than just for guarding. I note from John Cree's book *Understanding the German Shepherd Dog* (also published by The Crowood Press), that they have successfully been used as a 'Seeing Eye' breed in the USA in much the same way that retrievers are used as guide dogs in the UK.

However, just as certain attributes or traits are keenly sought by the professional organizations, they can also cause havoc and dismay when misdirected or wrongly used in a nervous dog. A German Shepherd Dog that has suffered from one or more major adverse behaviour-influencing factors (or worse still a combination of all of them) will often display antisocial behaviour beyond the control of ordinary dog owners. The breed's strengths, which normally provide a means for its gainful employment, can also very quickly become a liability for some owners. Nervous dogs can soon become over enthusiastic about defending the home, the surrounding gardens and boundaries (perceived to be their human-canine pack's territory) and can be aggressive towards owners, other dogs and complete strangers.

German Shepherds are known to form extremely powerful bonds with individuals. In

This trained police dog, Hobbs, is responding to a command by his handler to display aggression. For almost a century, the world's armed forces, police and prison services have utilized the German Shepherd Dog for the breed's instinct, strength and aggressive traits.

PC Gareth Dixon and his dog, Nelson. The strong bond between handler and dog enables them to work as a team. The police dog has to be intelligent and disciplined to correctly respond to instructions given in difficult circumstances.

some cases, this behaviour can be described as hyper-attachment, and it is one that can lead to canine separation-related disorders and a range of status-seeking dominance- and fear-aggression-driven behaviours. This aspect of the German Shepherd, which is definitely not breed-specific, is discussed in some depth within the pages of this book.

The effects of any combination of the ten major behaviour-influencing factors (*see* box right) can turn the German Shepherd into a creature that a human with a dog phobia would describe as their worst nightmare.

The Companion Dog

A happy and healthy German Shepherd Dog can, without any doubt, make the perfect companion animal. Its almost iconic characteristics – energy, power, bravery, faithfulness, intelligence and intuitive understanding – explain why this dog has dominated the Kennel Club's top-breed registration lists decade after decade. For those dog lovers who want the ultimate companion pet, this wonderful breed can certainly fulfil a dream.

By contrast, there are owners whose agenda for keeping a German Shepherd are somewhat disconcerting. Some want a powerful guard dog in the home, some want an aggressive protector, and there are those who want to project the threat of 'wolf' to others. The breed can fit into both 'companion' and 'guard dog' camps very easily. But it is this paradox that can be the undoing for many people in the owner–GSD partnership. I believe that an owner and family must decide which dog personality they truly desire. If a family pet is desired then all forms of guarding and aggression must be eliminated – through training. This must be done calmly, without any aggression on the part of the owner. A companion dog must trust his owner, and aggression from an abusing owner can only bring out aggression in the dog.

Antisocial and problem behaviour: ten major influences

These negative influences commonly occur when the dog is very young, but they are by no means confined to puppyhood. Many of them can just as easily affect adult dogs.

- Poor litter and early socialization (the first six to twelve weeks), including early removal from the litter, a nervous litter mother, extended stay with the litter mother, and social isolation (from other dogs and from human interaction).
- Excessive competition between siblings or older dogs in large litters or mixed age groups.
- Any experience of trauma or intrusive surgery.
- Temperament problems in one or both of the parent dogs.
- Abuse or mishandling by owners.
- Inappropriate or incomplete diet, starvation or undernourishment.
- Attacks or aggressive domination by other dogs.
- The puppy is the result of an accidental mating, and there is poor aftercare.
- Faulty learning where the puppies have experienced nervous and/or aggressive behaviour with little or no provocation from an adult dog.
- Poor physical health.

If a family decides their priority is for a guard dog then control, muzzling and reduced companionship will be the order of the day. Most families desire a pet that can be trusted with anyone from the youngest child to the new stranger and all other dogs. It is possible to promote calm behaviour in a family pet who will then show gentle behaviour to the smallest child and even to the most boisterous dog. But it is equally possible to promote aggression simply by following the training methods of those organizations that wish to harness this aspect of the German Shepherd personality.

Bess, at nine months, is thriving in her rural environment with a group of adult German Shepherd Dogs. If we could ask a German Shepherd where he would like to live I'm sure he would reply that a 'rural setting and a large garden with a warm home' would be 'most excellent'. However, a 'town dog' kept in a small house with only a backyard, even in the most urban setting, can be happy with daily pavement walks and regular weekend excursions to the nearest dog-friendly parks, fields and forests.

A Large Dog with a Strong Personality

There are both genetic and environmental influences that can create two different types of German Shepherd. The dominant individual will challenge and test his owner; the passive individual will follow every instruction to the letter and would not in any circumstances consider challenging his pack-leader and owner. The real problem is that when they are juvenile and still coming to terms with the absence of the litter mother, siblings and humans that they have interacted with during their young lives, it is almost impossible to ascertain which of a group of puppies is genetically predisposed to becoming one type or the other.

Whichever type of puppy an owner buys it is important to realize that an adult German Shepherd Dog requires strong leadership, training, and a minimum 3 to 5km (2–3 mile) daily walk combining lead and some freestyle (off-lead) exercise (*see* Chapter 4). It has been written that people in small homes or apartments should not keep large dogs, but I believe that provided good, healthy walks are offered on a daily basis – come rain or shine – then it is possible to own a large breed and not own a big home. It is snobbish for authors to write that only those who live in the rural or semi-rural countryside, with a medium to large home, should keep working and large breeds. Yes, that environment could be thought of as ideal, but I've known country folk who barely walk their dogs. However, it is not always practical to keep a large dog in a small, 'people-busy' home whether it is a rural or urban location. It is therefore the environment rather than the specific location that must be considered before taking on a German Shepherd Dog.

Some large German Shepherd individuals stand level at a tall person's hip height, and these dogs can be strong willed and physically powerful. Without psychological control, such a dog can be very physically intimidating and immediately 'in your face' almost before you have even had a chance to give an instruction or sit down on the settee. To prevent this antisocial behaviour from excluding all but your bravest and most dog-loving friends and family members from your home, it is necessary to be able to firmly control your dog at a single command. Training a German Shepherd from the earliest puppy stage is absolutely vital for a good long-term relationship. It is one matter to have an untrained puppy, playfully leap-ing up at family members and friends, and another altogether to have a huge, uncontrollable dog hurling himself at them.

There are many myths about pet keeping. One is that an owner must be a dog's 'master' by *physically* showing him who is the 'boss'. This is the approach taken by a human that is predisposed to bullying and abusive behaviour. There is a huge difference between being a dog's respected leader and being his tyrannical ruler. A large dog with a strong personality needs the former, never the latter. The same principle can be applied to many other spheres of animal training. For example, it is possible to 'break' a horse by physically intimidating it and terrifying it into submission; but it is also possible – and far more desirable – to 'train' it by gaining its willing submission, which can be done only by earning its respect and confidence. This latter system of training is based on the positive reinforcement of good behaviour rather than the direct punishment of bad. Positive reinforcement requires the use of reward, which can vary from food or a chance to play with a toy, to a pat and/or vocal congratulation. Once a dog has learned the basic commands, and simple instructions can be fully associated and understood, good behaviour should become ingrained.

Some trainers don't believe that any reward for basic obedience is necessary. They would argue that it is enough for a puppy or a dog to understand he has accomplished the right task or responded in the correct manner. As a parent, as a dog owner, as a husband and as a psychologist, I can confidently state that we all enjoy being 'rewarded' for our kindness, our efforts and good behaviour. It is proven through clinical research that positive reinforcement works successfully in both humans and dogs. Ask a parent with a child being treated for attention-deficit disorder, and ask any qualified animal behaviourist how they would go about promoting better

German Shepherds need mental and physical training, grooming, daily walks, and a good-quality diet. When all these important needs are consistently fulfilled, this large breed with the strong personality will be happy, healthy, and a perfect companion animal.

behaviour from an over-enthusiastic or hyperactive dog. Understanding the principles of training are essential when taking on a dog. But it is especially important when dealing with a large, powerful dog like the German Shepherd.

3   Becoming a German Shepherd Dog Owner

The major commitment involved in keeping any large, working-breed dog cannot be understated. However, it is not always easy to focus on this important factor when first viewing a delightful litter of puppies. These fluffy, endearing, warm-blooded youngsters are quite simply living teddy bears. Interacting with puppies is therapeutic in that repeatedly stroking them lowers our heart rate and blood pressure levels and, when they are not biting or going to the toilet in the wrong places, their company can reduce our stress levels.

However, puppies rapidly grow and develop into much larger animals. A German Shepherd puppy needs daily grooming and walking, after the necessary inoculations have been arranged, and daily feeding for, on average, 12 years. Those walks have to be taken in all conditions – sunny, snowy, wet and windy (or even in a combination of all weathers in the UK). My father brought me up to accept this as a daily responsibility if I was ever to keep my own dog.

I am not exactly sure anyone is completely qualified to declare who should and who shouldn't own a German Shepherd Dog because I am not happy with generalizations on this subject. The ideal owner would probably be described in most breed books as one who is fit and healthy and who has both the home space for a large dog breed and the time and effort required to train and walk a potentially powerful pet on a daily basis. The physical strength and power of an adult GSD suggests that anyone of an unhealthy or infirm disposition should avoid the breed. The other important deciding factor is the relatively high cost of keeping and maintaining an adult German Shepherd. This does represent a significant amount of money and so it is sensible to be sure that you, as a responsible owner, are able to afford to feed and maintain one.

Even the author finds that these living teddy bears are at this age impossible to resist.

The GSD owner must be committed to providing the general care, training, and daily outdoor exercise that this large, intelligent breed requires. Here, Bess enjoys the outdoors with GSD breeder and show judge Marian.

Faulty learning

The term faulty learning is used by animal behaviourists to describe the cause of anti-social behaviour associated with the process of development, especially during the early socialization period (the first one to twelve weeks of life). During this period it is possible for puppies to develop bad habits. Exposure to adverse situations and environments, poor diet or displays of antisocial behaviours, such as aggression by the litter mother or other dogs, other animals and humans, will significantly influence the behavioural development of a puppy, teaching it that it is acceptable behaviour to direct aggression towards other dogs, innocent strangers or inappropriate targets. Any fragmentation or interruption, such as early removal from the litter mother and siblings (before six weeks), during this period can also adversely affect a puppy's behaviour.

The litter mother in effect lays the foundations for later training. She teaches the puppies to urinate and defecate away from the nest area, and she also teaches important aspects of social behaviour, such as bite inhibition and controlling demands for attention. From the negative reactions and yelp signalling from the litter mother, siblings, and other adult dogs, puppies learn that biting and excessive mouthing is antisocial behaviour. If a puppy is removed early from the litter, problem behaviours such as aggression, over-dependency, mental detachment and inappropriate toileting usually develop and become progressive conditions unless treated.

Having decided that you wish to become a German Shepherd owner, and that you are prepared to accept the responsibility it entails, you will have to determine whether to buy a puppy or to re-home an adult dog or older puppy. For most people, obtaining a new puppy is the wisest course, and this chapter will explain what is involved in finding, and caring for, your young companion. Some of the information will also be relevant to the care and management of an older dog, but since there are additional factors that must be taken into account when re-homing or 'rescuing' a German Shepherd, this subject is dealt with separately in Chapter 5.

Finding the Right Puppy

The most important factor is to know where to obtain a German Shepherd puppy. If you want to shorten the odds on buying a happy, correctly socialized dog, then avoid inexperienced home breeders that are out to make money, puppy farms, commercial kennels, large stores or small pet shops and farms. This should seem obvious, but not everyone is aware of, or informed about, these places, which have inadvertently provided my behaviour clinic with hundreds of 'patients'

The litter mother socializes her puppies from birth. She teaches them by reacting firmly to any overdemanding, mouthing or biting behaviour. These three newborn puppies will give their mother, Remy, few problems at this time as they are blind and deaf and completely dependent on her for the first three weeks of life, a development stage known as the reflex period.

during the past decade. The reason why these sources of puppies produce 'problem pets' is primarily that in all of these environments puppies will usually show signs of faulty learning, where the litter is not shown important aspects of socialization (*see* box, opposite). Puppies may experience poor and interrupted socialization when they are removed from the litter mother too early (whole litters change hands for money and are then moved) or when litters of mixed ages are placed together. Whelping conditions are often appalling. Puppies are also likely to be from poor stock, the result of breeding 'sad' animals with terrible antisocial temperaments. Nervous and aggressive litter mothers produce nervous and aggressive puppies.

Adverse events, such as trauma or aggression shown by other dogs or owners during the early stages of a puppy's life, can trigger or encourage the later development of fear and dominance behaviours. Fear and nervous aggression behaviour can also be linked to the early removal of a puppy from the litter. Long-term kennel dogs, 'singleton' puppies, large-litter puppies, badly handled dogs and puppies are all known to develop problem behaviours. Those puppies that originate from working stock (farms, police kennels and guard-dog trainers, and so on) will probably experience certain aggressive and territorial behaviours during the socialization period. A dog from the police kennels will have been 'rejected' as unsuitable for training. If you want a companion pet, these puppies will not represent the ideal stock.

It is of course possible to buy a difficult puppy from an experienced, professional

Remy's 'Magnificent Seven' line up for the last photograph in the week before they go to their new homes. It is advisable to view puppies when they are between six and seven weeks old before making a final selection.

Judith and Catherine watch the puppies in action and look for a bright, alert individual. It can be difficult to choose one puppy over another, and it can be very difficult to be objective. In many cases it is the puppy that 'chooses' his owner.

breeder. Sometimes the 'show dogs' used for breeding stock are dominant individuals, especially the sire or male dogs. If at all possible find someone at a breed club who can introduce you to an adult dog that has a strong, yet calm, gentle nature. The temperament of such a dog speaks volumes for the breeder and owner and gives you a starting point for finding your puppy.

The Right Age

Among animal behaviourists, the current thinking regarding the ideal age to bring a puppy home is that it should not be removed from its litter mother and siblings beyond ten weeks old or under six weeks old. A puppy removed from the litter under six weeks of age will miss out on essential aspects of the socialization process and will therefore often suffer in terms of the development of social skills. As we have seen, these life-skills for puppies are learned and experienced through general interaction with the litter mother and siblings, including play and feeding, in the first weeks following birth.

If a puppy is taken from the litter *after* ten weeks it will have developed some attachment to the dogs and humans that share its environment. This means that there is potentially a relationship dependency with its litter mother and any remaining siblings. There may also be a strong attachment to the humans with which a puppy has had regular contact. When these early-bond relationships are severed there can be side-effects or behavioural problems such as separation-related disorder, introverted, withdrawn behaviour, or extrovert hyperactivity. The ideal mother-to-puppy socialization-development period is somewhere between the six and eight weeks stages. Removal during this period should ensure a healthy puppy avoids developing behavioural problems linked to socialization interruption.

In an ideal situation, the breeder will have taken every opportunity to expose the puppies to the outside world. A litter of puppies that has been well socialized will usually have encountered a wide range of aspects of home life. This might include interacting with adult dogs with good temperaments and becoming familiar with other pets, such as a cat, rabbit or guinea pig. They will have been for a couple of short car trips and have been handled by a steady stream of children and adults. If you can find a breeder who has cheerfully undertaken these simple aspects of puppy socialization then put your name down for your new companion pet.

Choosing a Puppy

There has been a great deal of nonsense written about the subject of selecting a puppy, and this has ranged from the means by which you should decide on the gender to the methods of choosing the ideal individual for a specific purpose. The most common advice is that the potential buyer should always assess the mother and, ideally, the sire, and should assess all the puppies in the litter to determine which is the most suitable. However, it is often difficult to observe mother and pups beyond a brief period, and even more difficult to fully profile the personality of the breeding male and his pedigree line. And it is extremely difficult to be even remotely objective when viewing a chaotic group of puppies. They are all delightful. It's true that sometimes a special individual stands out; it might be something to do with his colour, or it may be another appealing physical aspect such as the ears, eyes, nose, tail and so on. Sometimes the thing that hooks a person is a particular behaviour or perceived personality characteristic. In a group of puppies there might be the shy type, the mischievous boy, the individual full of bravado, the cocky one that nonchalantly wees on your shoe, or the

The choice is made and a new relationship begins to form.

individual that nibbles your shoelaces or even your finger. Then again, your puppy might be the only one that is unsold at the time of your visit!

Choosing the sex of your puppy is also inexorably linked to some rather subjective influences. My parents always kept several generations of Boxer bitches and, in complete opposition, I have kept only male Boxer dogs. The general facts are that male dogs can sometimes show a fervent desire to roam and seek out the opposite sex. Male dogs are more driven to frequent marking of territory with urine and faeces. Keeping a male dog means that you do not have to worry about seasons as you do with a bitch, who will come on heat twice a year. A bitch may discharge blood in the wrong places in

a home and will attract neighbourhood male dogs by the dozen. Bitches in season have to be isolated during the ten- to fourteen-day period from rampant male dogs.

One generalization has it that female dogs are likely to be more passive than males, that they don't like to wander, and that they are less likely to become dominant and challenge owners. Male dogs can be more challenging but they also make powerful bonds and follow consistent leadership from owners. It is also said that male dogs are more likely to display protective-possessive-territorial types of aggressive behaviours. However, dominant German Shepherd bitches can be just as bossy and as much trouble to handle as dominant male dogs.

Attempt to observe the puppies at different times rather than on just one occasion because you may be viewing the puppies in a particular mode of behaviour. This might be when they are sleepy or when they have just been fed or when they are hyperactive or in a frustrated mood.

Once you have decided on your puppy, it is always a good idea to visit the breeder on several occasions before the day arrives to take your puppy home (although your viewing opportunities will depend on how busy the breeder is and how much access he or she offers). Repeat visits should enable you to get to know the breeder, see the litter mother and, most importantly, observe the puppies at different times. Meeting the litter mother more than once will give you a chance to confirm that she has a good personality.

If the puppies are being cared for in a home environment then it is likely that they will be first-stage house-trained and accustomed to regular human interaction. If the puppies are maintained in an outdoor pen they are more likely to need specific house-training because the easy-to-clean concrete run outside the sheltered area is usually used as the communal toilet. Pen-contained puppies will tend to receive the most attention during feeding or cleaning out times, or when people come to view or select a puppy, and this can give rise to the development of contact-sensitivity or association in puppies. This is when the puppy does not easily understand human interaction outside of feeding or cleaning.

Collecting Your New Puppy

On the big day (if you are reading this with an adult German Shepherd by your side this may seem a long time ago), it is best to be fully prepared. Most breeders will provide a current diet sheet with recommendations, and they will be happy to offer you a sample of food and some basic feeding and caring guidance. Do your best to create the minimum amount of fuss with your chosen puppy. The puppy will be frightened and emotional and physical security is paramount to his welfare. However exciting or romantic it may seem, it is not advisable to transport a puppy clutched in your arms or blanketed on your knee. Instead use a purpose-made wire or plastic, formed carrier, or an economical cardboard carrier that can be obtained from most pet shops. Even a stout cardboard box, lined with an old towel, can become a 'den' or place of safety for a nervous puppy travelling for the first time.

It is highly recommended that this first important journey is made with a family member or friend so that one person is totally free to look after the needs of the puppy whilst the other drives. This car journey for your puppy will probably be his first encounter with the big wide world outside his original home. Be prepared for whimpering,

The puppy's first days with his new owner are both unsettling and exciting. If you have made several visits to the breeder, you and your puppy will already have started to get to know each other.

crying or even howling. Although a confident puppy will probably take the whole transfer, from breeder to your home, in his stride, some puppies may be travel sick. In the first instance nausea is indicated by slavering, but this may culminate in the bringing up of a small amount of undigested food. I have known some nervous individuals completely regurgitate their last meal in reaction to the trauma of the car journey. With this possibility firmly in mind, it is best to be fully prepared: arm yourself with baby wipes, kitchen roll and even a spare blanket or towel. With an almost military-style operation in mind, attempt to make the journey as problem- and fuss-free as possible for your puppy.

Creating the Right Environment

A German Shepherd puppy requires a pre-formed nylon or basket bed or, better still, a folding travel crate (indoor kennel), and a set of robust feeding and drinking bowls. Some owners have found puppy pens a blessing when there is a need to restrict a puppy's movements in the first six months. An indoor, fenced-off area can be a boon when you have a number of guests or a group of children running around a home in excited party mood. Needless to say, it is essential that you acquire all the necessary equipment before you go to collect your puppy.

Once your puppy is home, the settling-in period can begin. It is important that the puppy has a place to rest and to feel safe and secure. The puppy's crate or folding indoor kennel should be covered at the top (purpose-made covers are best) and base-lined with a favourite blanket or a purpose-sized bed. The crate can be used to confine your puppy overnight or for limited random periods. The security offered by the crate, which represents a den, bolt-hole, lair or burrow to

your puppy, will often help to eliminate any distress-related problems such as destructive behaviour and inappropriate urination or defecation.

The bed or crate should be placed in a draught-free position to prevent shivers, and it should also be away from bedrooms and living rooms as this will help to reduce the potential for dependency on the constant presence of people.

It is ideal if the crate is collapsible and able to fit into your vehicle. Motoring organizations recommend the use of travel crates as many dogs are killed each year following road traffic accidents when the back of the vehicle or a passenger door opens and a dog is unfortunately released onto a motorway or a busy road and is immediately disorientated. If a covered crate is to be used for travelling in the car it is important to remove the cover and to ensure proper ventilation during warm weather. (Of course, in hot, or even warm conditions a dog must never be left in a car – in a crate or otherwise.)

Do not encourage your puppy to access stairs or to sleep in your bedroom or on your bed as this could lead to challenging behaviour or may encourage over-dependency in the dog. As the puppy grows, allowing bedroom access may have greater implications, such as sleep disruption, the shedding of hairs (a greater problem in a adult dog), and general disobedience.

A stair-gate will prevent your puppy from climbing the stairs. This is a recommendation that is not made simply to prevent injury. Height has great significance for a dog: the dominant animal in a pack will always occupy the vantage point, the most elevated place in an area, whether this happens to be a platform, such as a log or rock-ledge or boulder, or merely a natural rise in the ground level. Restricting your dog's ability to assume height is therefore an important factor in control. By allowing a dog to

Most puppies become very attached to the indoor kennel or crate, treating it as a den and continuing to use it as a haven throughout their adult lives.

occupy elevated positions you are inadvertently giving him a psychological advantage. My clinical records show that bites to members of the family often occur when the dog is on the stairs, either when the dog is startled during sleep, or because the dog is displaying nervous, dominant and possessive behaviour associated with protecting a vantage point. A raised position on the stairs, or even on the bed, gives the dog status, and this will encourage the dog to guard the platform and, in extreme instances, use it as a springboard for attack.

Early Days

The initial 24 hours will probably be the most difficult period for your puppy. For your new companion, a new life and home means adapting to a strange environment with unfamiliar sights and smells. Few puppies are deliriously happy on the first night and there will be some crying or even howling as your puppy mourns the separation from his mother and siblings. Do not be tempted to over-fuss or give excessive attention to your puppy in this phase or the attention-seeking crying or whining behaviour will be encouraged to the point that it will occur every time separation happens. In the following weeks the puppy will settle down and his mother and siblings will be forgotten as his new life becomes more and more exciting.

The initial handling strategy needs to be one of little fuss and limited stroking and petting. You will feel an instinctive need to reassure young GSD that everything's OK, but if you keep this to a minimum your puppy's natural curiosity in his new surroundings will come to the fore and he will gradually come out of his shell. Your love and attention is of course needed to replace the litter mother's instinctive care, but canine adoption is most successfully achieved when it is done with realistic handling and consistency in controlled contact.

It is important to allow a puppy peaceful periods of rest. It can be stressful to disrupt a puppy's sleep. Inactive periods should not be interrupted simply because a member of the family wants to play with the new puppy. All puppies need a quiet place to rest if positive behavioural and growth developments are to be made. There are also times in every

---

Indoor kennels or crates: ten top tips

If the crate is to be useful to you and at the same time a place of security and comfort for your dog, his experience of using the crate must be positive. To ensure that this is the case, follow these guidelines.

1. Confinement of your dog in the crate should *never* be used as a punishment.

2. The crate must be covered to create the den effect.

3. The crate should be just large enough for your puppy to stand up and lie down in. This will ensure it is used for relaxation and rest – not exercise! A restricted size also discourages leaping up or barking at passers-by.

4. Place the crate in a quiet corner of the home, away from visual contact with family members coming and going.

5. The crate should not be used for visits to the vet (at least not in the early days) as this represents a potentially negative experience. It should be used if you move house, travel, caravan, boat, or when taking your puppy to other homes or premises.

6. Place your puppy's bedding inside and leave the crate door open. Introduce your puppy to the crate with the minimum of fuss. Ideally, leave the puppy in the room where you have placed the crate and step away to allow natural exploration. If the puppy should ignore the crate, secretly place an enticing bone or novel toy inside and give your puppy time and privacy to discover the bone and his new 'den'.

7. The best period to experiment with the crate is night-time when the puppy is naturally relaxing and ready to rest. Allow at least a week for a natural introduction if possible. The more relaxed and confident your puppy is when entering and leaving the folding crate, the better.

8. Place an item of your old clothing inside the crate (re-scent the item by leaving it in your washing basket or wearing it overnight or for a day) to encourage your puppy to explore the unit. This item then represents a comfort blanket.

9. To begin with, random crating is best as this will avoid any negative association. If your puppy is placed into the crate only when 'exciting' events occur (when visitors arrive, for example) he will be reluctant to go in the den and may become frustrated and distressed when restrained inside. Create a timetable for half-hour sessions during the day and at weekends to get your puppy used to going into his den.

10. Place your puppy inside before visitors arrive and release him while they are still at your home. If your puppy is quietly resting inside, occasionally 'click and treat' him (*see* page 49) to reward this good behaviour and to create a positive association with crating.

---

busy family week when an adventurous and curious puppy will be under foot or too hyperactive to cope with guests. Sometimes it is very useful to be able to restrain your puppy without developing or increasing his frustration. It is in these situations that the crate can prove especially valuable.

Proper use of the crate is essential if you are to ensure the puppy does not develop any negative associations with it (*see* box, above). If, having followed these guidelines, your puppy shows little interest in entering the crate (after several daytime and overnight periods) then it is important that you are firm and instruct him or her to enter. Gently, but firmly, back your puppy into the crate and close the door. Leave the puppy alone for a brief period (five to ten minutes) and return. Open the door, praise calmness, and allow the puppy to exit of his own accord. Repeat this over the day and for the last period at night.

House-training

Your German Shepherd puppy should be restricted to one area in your home for the first week. Newspapers can be placed on the floor between the puppy's sleeping place and an outside access door. Your puppy will soon need to investigate your home but this can be gradually permitted when you are confident that toilet accidents, which often come as a result of nervousness in a new home environment, are down to a minimum.

It is important to praise and reward your puppy with a stroke and a food treat *immediately* you observe him using the paper. There is no point in delivering the reward long after the event, as he will not understand why you are pleased with him. It is therefore wise to be especially alert at the times the puppy is most likely to want to relieve himself: immediately after sleep or a short interactive play, or in the half-hour period after eating. Remember also that any shouting or attempts to punish your puppy for any failures or mistakes will simply confuse him.

If the weather is reasonable in the first days of the home-coming, a puppy can be introduced into the garden. Transfer a soiled paper into the garden to encourage urination and defecation in a chosen toilet area. Once again, always reward your puppy for using this area. With care, promotion from newspapers to an appropriate toilet place will take less than a week to achieve.

Food and Water

A bowl of clean water should be available at all times. (Tap water and rainwater as an organic mix, filtered through aquarium filter wool or a cloth and served at room temperature, is excellent.) A food dish should be made available only at meal times. When it is feeding time, place a clean dish of food down for your puppy. Once you have started using the 'clicker' system (*see* Chapter 4) you should click as you place the dish down to signal that the food is part of the reward system.

Your puppy will soon realize that when you bring the dish out it is time to eat. Ideally, the dish should be removed as soon as the puppy walks away. This will emphasize your control. When the puppy has finished eating, it is important to allow him to rest and properly digest his food.

Three small meals of as much as your puppy can eat in about five minutes (ten minutes maximum), should be spread evenly across the day and given after a walk or play session. Follow the breeder's diet guidelines: do not be tempted to change the diet in the first few days as this can cause digestive upset, which will be exacerbated by the stress of being in a new environment. Any change that you do eventually implement should be done very gradually.

Chewing

Your home is likely to be filled with inappropriate targets that should not be chewed. There are electrical wires, furniture legs, soft furnishings, shoes and house plants, to name just a few. Redirect your puppy's need to chew to appropriate items. For example, make a hard, durable toy or hide chew or an uncooked, natural bone available for your puppy to 'discover' as he explores a new area in your home. Once the 'clicker' system is in place (*see* Chapter 4) you can signal that the chew is an appropriate target for this behaviour. Much better than your trousers, shoes and fingers! This strategy means that a puppy will choose to chew designated targets over dangerous and expensive items. Introducing basic training at an early age will teach your puppy good social manners and reduce elements of boredom. When they are young German Shepherd puppies are

Castration and spaying

Your puppy becomes a fully mature, adult dog between 12 and 18 months of age. During this period his physical and hormonal development peaks and he reaches sexual maturity. It is at this stage that in nature – in packs of wild dogs or wolves – a dog finds his place within the pack structure.

If you do not intend to breed from your dog, castration or spaying is recommended. The surgery usually takes place between the ages of 6 and 12 months or (in the case of a bitch) after the first season. Neutering will not treat the majority of behavioural problems, but there are some cases that may benefit, such as dogs or bitches with a tendency to wander. In dogs it will suppress the desire to chase after bitches or to display inappropriate sexual behaviour (towards the legs of humans for example); in bitches it will prevent phantom pregnancy and, if done early enough, reduces the risk of mammary tumours and pyometra. It is known to take up to six months for a neutered dog's hormonal levels to fully subside.

very willing to learn and they respond to rewarded sessions.

To prevent the development of obsessive-compulsive chewing behaviour, natural bones or chews should be available for only short ten- to fifteen-minute periods. If your puppy has a brief chew and eventually walks away from an item then it is important that it is removed immediately. If your puppy continues to chew beyond the recommended period, use distraction (offer another toy or food treat at a short distance away) so that you can remove the item and prevent any potential displays of 'possessive' or competitive challenge or aggression.

First Visit to the Vet

Your new puppy should be examined as early as possible by a veterinary surgeon. The vet will give him a general check-up and also start the vaccination programme, which is es-

sential to protect your puppy from contracting diseases from other dogs. The diseases are: canine distemper, canine leptospirosis (or Weil's disease), canine parvovirus, and infectious canine hepatitis. Depending on the circumstances, vaccination against kennel cough may also be given. Vaccination is normally administered in two separate injections given about ten days apart when the puppy is between the ages of six and ten weeks. You should not take your puppy out for walks or allow contact with other dogs outside the home until the vaccination programme is complete.

Treatment for worms (*see* Chapter 7) is also essential, and continues to be so at regular intervals throughout the adult dog's life. The first and second worming treatments are given within a fortnight of each other at three and six weeks of age.

This first veterinary check-up allows early detection of any physical problems, which can be very important as many conditions will respond well to prompt treatment but less positively if they are allowed to worsen. After an inspection your vet should be able to give your puppy a 'clean bill of health' and offer you further advice on worming and flea treatments.

Use a pet carrier to safely transport your puppy to the veterinary clinic. Offer your puppy a small food treat while waiting in the surgery and another following the examination. The veterinary surgery is a potentially bewildering (and frightening) environment, so do all you can to make the experience as positive as possible.

Grooming

Your puppy should be briefly groomed on a daily basis to encourage a positive association with brushing the dog's coat and also to allow a cursory health-check session. Use a firm brush, and follow up with combing.

This family found themselves with puppies after their rescue GSD-cross was accidentally mated. Puppies are a great responsibility, and early-age neutering should be considered for most family pets.

Gently brush the coat and underbelly. It is a good idea to lay a white cloth underneath your puppy to catch any debris that could indicate flea infestations and so on. Offer a food reward, such as a dog treat, for your puppy's good obedience and attention especially when he is in the Sit or Stand position.

Use this five-minute session to check your puppy all over. Look carefully into the mouth, and check the eyes, ears and nose for any discharge. Wipe these carefully with a damp cloth. A dampened dog towel can be used to wipe down your puppy if he has been up to mischief, such as standing in his own waste, rooting in plant pots, or slipping and sliding through muddy ground.

Always check the anal area for any tell-tale signs of sloppy faeces. Any unusual indications should be discussed with a veterinary nurse at the earliest opportunity. Loose stools may simply indicate a temporarily upset tummy but if encountered repeatedly they could indicate a more serious problem.

Your puppy will quickly accept an examination and grooming session as part of your relationship. You may occasionally need to bath your puppy but this should be undertaken carefully (*see* Chapter 7).

Socialization

Other Dogs and Family Pets

Introducing a new puppy to an older dog has to be undertaken carefully. Few happy and healthy adult dogs will attack or show aggression towards a puppy, but the introduction has to be taken slowly and sensibly. An existing dog or cat will consider your home to be his territory – something to be defended. Most breeders would introduce new pets to existing home animals on a walk or on near-by neutral ground.

Any aggression from your existing animal should be discouraged, and controls should be in place. An older dog being introduced to a younger dog should be encouraged to play or exercise in an activity both animals can enjoy.

Any early interaction should take place in a neutral area (field, garden, on a walk) and

A puppy that has been brought up with the experience of interacting with different people, including children, has the best chance of becoming a much-loved and valued family pet. However, floor play with children can confuse a puppy and, ideally, should be controlled.

humans should detach themselves but be able to control dogs should any problems occur. All food should be kept away from the meeting; and for the first few days meals should be offered separately. Once there is full acceptance of the newcomer by the existing pet then meals can be offered in separate dishes at the same time.

Many veterinary clinics hold socialization classes for puppies, which can be attended in the weeks following the post-vaccination period. These sessions allow you to introduce your puppy to other puppies, which will help reduce hyperactivity and any potential for aggressive behaviour towards other dogs in later life. Puppy classes can also be informative in that most veterinary nurses can offer advice and answer some of the questions you may have regarding your puppy.

It is possible to progress from these introduction sessions to socialization classes with older dogs where basic obedience training and control can be gradually implemented. Your local vet can usually advise you on both puppy classes and training schools.

Healthy and happy puppies will usually mix with almost any animal because they are more adaptable than adult dogs. Their associations with many aspects of life are still to be formed. There are many homes where a dog and cat sprawl out together by the fireside. In the early months there is a natural curiosity between animals, which gives rise to mutual inspection. Instinctive behaviour (based on the predator/prey relationship) can lead to a dog chasing a rabbit, or a cat chasing a bird (in which case the various animals should be maintained separately). But, in general, animals accept their co-habitees, even if they do not tolerate that species outside of the home. For example, some dogs will get on with their 'own' cat but attempt to chase others.

Owner/Puppy Interaction
Play, interaction and exploration are important factors in a puppy's social development period. During a waking cycle your puppy will display alternate spells of activity and sleep. Puppies need to explore, interact, chew, eat, urinate and defecate. Your interaction should be in short five-minute sessions in order to prevent hyperactivity and over-excitement. Try to avoid rough and tumble types of play because this behaviour is less appropriate when your puppy is older.

If complete supervision of your puppy is not possible during the active periods it is best to restrict a puppy's movements. If yours is a hectic home with a busy family it may be useful to use a puppy pen. In good weather, providing there is shade from direct sunlight provided, this can be temproraily installed in the garden. Indoors, the pen can be used to reduce the area your puppy can wander around in whilst allowing individual play.

There are times when your puppy should rest and be comfortable and independent away from the family. It is not ideal, and certainly not necessary, to have a 'shadow' companion because this type of dog can quickly become totally dependent on you. For such a dog, periods of enforced separation – while you are at work, school, college or during holidays, and so on – will make him nervous and insecure. To promote your leadership, and to ensure that your puppy develops into a confident and independent adult dog, it is

necessary to consider important aspects of controlling, walking, playing and feeding.

For owners who are always at home, I recommend the drawing up of a 'time table of home separation times' during the day and evenings. About 50 per cent of the time (in hour or half-hour periods) there should be no visual or physical contact with the family outside of walks and play interactions. This strategy will promote independent and calm behaviour.

If members of the family are at work or education during the day it still remains important to build up separation or time-out periods. This can help to reduce the contrast between your presence and absence and prevent over-dependency. A talk radio programme in the background before during and after your return, can offer a replacement for the comforting sound of humans.

Interaction with puppies should always be brief and undemanding as it is possible to promote hyperactivity through extended play sessions.

When dogs attempt to lick our faces they are expressing submission and also looking to exchange scents.

Always ensure that your dog does not jump up at you or your visitors and others (*see* Chapter 4). Again, consistent handling from the early days is important. If a dog believes he is 'required' to be highly excited whenever you return home, or whenever guests arrive, then this is exactly the behaviour that will be promoted. It is one matter for a cuddly puppy to display enthusiasm at your return or at the arrival of guests, but it is quite another to have an adult German Shepherd Dog confronting you or them.

It is also possible to promote calm behaviour from your puppy on your exit or entrance by ignoring excitable behaviour and rewarding positive behaviour with your attention and a sequence of click and treats (*see* Chapter 4).

Pack Hierarchy

In the wild, a 'top dog', referred to by canine researchers as the alpha male (or female),

is in control of the pack. In domestication, this pack structure continues to exist but in an adapted form: what I refer to as the 'human–canine pack'. A developing puppy needs to understand his place within this adapted social structure: that you and your family are the leaders. Your puppy should look for your guidance on walks and in the home. This understanding of pack position in a strong-willed breed such as a German Shepherd is vital and requires an owner to be assertive and committed to training.

In the wild, pack hierarchy is maintained vigorously by the alpha dog beating off any leadership challenge from individuals both from within the pack and from outside it. This need to dominate subordinates is most apparent at breeding times, when young animals that have become fully grown try their luck against the leader. In domesticated dog terms, this is the period when behaviours related to mating – such as wandering, and challenging and possessive aggressions – are at their peak. Research suggests that bitches have the higher status in nature and in domestication.

For the human leader, control at this adolescent stage needs to be psychological rather than physical. So it is important that you are able to interpret your dog's perception of the pack hierarchy and to recognize dominant and submissive behaviours. He will learn when to display dominant behaviour, and he will identify those to whom submissive behaviour has to be displayed. (*See* box, opposite.) This is important information to learn because once sexual maturity has been reached, aspects of social structure such as 'pack position' need to be clearly defined and established.

For example, a dog that lies down or maintains a position across a threshold is making a covert challenge. The dog wants you to try to move him and, when you attempt to argue over the position, a 'challenge' (growl, lunge or bite) can be made.

As mentioned earlier in this chapter, height is important to a dog. A dog that is attempting to raise his status with an owner will want to occupy the vantage positions in your home – the top or part way up the stairs, the chairs and furniture, and so on – and may show guarding and patrolling behaviour. It is important to your relationship with your young, rapidly developing dog that he is not allowed to assume these positions. Preventing these situations is easy providing the basic training begins early in the puppy stage.

By the same token, it is advisable not to lower yourself, or allow others, to descend to the puppy's height (i.e., avoid floor-level play and confrontations). This is because it is possible for you to inadvertently signal submissiveness on your part. Playing on the same level as your puppy may suggest that you are also a 'puppy', and that perception can result in challenges and confrontations at a later stage.

Play

The development of play is an important phase in canine development. In the wild, pack survival depends on co-operation in hunting and in rearing young. This in turn depends on the various members of the pack knowing their places. Play is important because it is one of the ways in which sibling rivalry can be expressed and in which the puppies can explore their relative positions in the pack. The social interaction and competition of play, mock-fighting, and tests of strength over the kill carcass, help to establish the sibling hierarchy.

The successful puppy learns which of his siblings can be made to back down and which have to be mollified. Submission and dominance are communicated through body language, which consists of a range of physical signals and body postures (*see* box, right).

The language of dominance and submission

For the dog pack to be successful, each member's status must be clearly defined and signalled to others. This requires a system of communication, which is based principally on body posturing, behaviour, and vocal sound. In all social interactions, the signals that a dog displays will be dictated by his perception of his position in the pack.

Dominant dog
- Moves smartly and purposefully towards other dogs.
- Stands erect, with head held up.
- Maintains direct eye contact.
- Raises the tail to the highest possible position.
- Raises hackles if challenge is anticipated.
- Marks territory by cocking the leg frequently and as high up as possible.
- Snarls: draws the lips up and back to expose upper teeth while narrowing the eyes.
- Growls or snaps in warning (as opposed to whining or whimpering).
- If necessary to prevent challenge, pins subordinate down by the scruff of the neck.

The overall impression created by a dog in dominant mode is of height and erectness above the ground.

Submissive dog
- Shuffles towards dominant dog, with body close to the ground and head bowed.
- Lies on the ground; may also turn over to expose belly.
- Avoids direct eye contact, and turns away from dominant dog.
- Lowers the tail, or even tucks it between the legs.
- Lowers the head to below shoulder level.
- Urinates whilst in submissive body posture.
- Grins: draws the lips down and back so that lower teeth are just visible. (Not to be confused with snarling, in which upper teeth are exposed and the eyes are narrowed.)
- Whines or whimpers in appeasement (as opposed to snarling or snapping).
- Licks the lower jaw of the dominant animal.

The overall impression created by a dog in submissive mode is of crouching or of bringing the body as low to the ground as possible.

Tug-of-war games teach a dog to test his strength against his owner and family. It is not advisable to develop these games with a German Shepherd Dog because they can encourage antisocial challenging behaviour.

you or a young family member as a fellow puppy during play. In these instances those needle-sharp teeth and scratching claws can become a nuisance or even dangerous. If your puppy bites or scratches at your hands or feet, say 'No' in a low tone (do not shout) and break off from play. Careful control will reinforce good behaviour. If play-biting is a problem you can introduce and use training discs (*see* Chapter 4, pages 53–4). Your puppy will eventually understand that good behaviour is rewarded while antisocial behaviour goes unrewarded.

It is important to emphasize that the best positive interactive play between you and your German Shepherd puppy is retrieval and foraging games as they promote submissive behaviour. Foraging games positively stimulate the psychological development of your puppy and permit instinctive behaviours that are under your control and on your terms. Simple versions of these games can even be introduced in the first few weeks of a puppy's new life with you.

Retrieval, selection or search-and-find games require hard rubber toys, and these should always be under your control and stored in a box away from your puppy.

First Outings
Marian Marsden, one of the main professional breeders with whom I have consulted during the writing of this book, points out that the period between a puppy's leaving the breeder, and the stage at which all necessary inoculations are complete at 12 weeks, is too long a time to wait before exposing a puppy to the 'big wide world'. She recommends that new owners take the puppy for brief visits to consenting family and friends. It is also useful to take the puppy on excursions to parks, woods and fields, provided you carry the puppy and do not allow him to walk on the ground in these environments. This type of activity will not only give the puppy new experiences but will expose the youngster to vehicle journeys and the general hubbub of the outside world.

Walks

I firmly believe that walks replace natural hunting and foraging episodes for dogs. This is especially true for working breeds, such as hounds and gundogs, where walks in a rural environment can provide an opportunity to 'work' if the dog is allowed to run free. Because they present opportunities for dogs to meet other dogs and to allow them to explore and sniff, scent and mark, walks represent the most exciting aspect of life's experience for all but the most timid dog.

In nature, hunting and foraging – or searching for food – takes up a great amount of time and energy for a dog or a wolf pack and, as such, much of a dog's natural behaviour is related to this task. Pack structure has its basis in group hunting. As an individual, a dog or a wolf is most likely to hunt opportunistically, and to be able to take only small birds and rodents. However, when canines work together in social groups or packs they are able to bring down and predate larger prey and therefore feed more pack members

and litters. Of course, in domestication, dogs do not actually hunt, but the need to embark on expeditions to explore the world and all its scents remains apparent.

Once your puppy's vaccinations are complete, it is possible to allow short, on-lead walk explorations in and around your neighbourhood. It is best to offer a series of short-distance walks rather than one long walk, as this will prevent overtiredness and potential hyperactivity from developing. You are bound to attact attention – people love puppies – but remember that too much contact and over-excitement can lead to stress-related problems.

Avoid using check-type collars, such as choke-chains, to control your dog on walks. These outdated forms of control bring your relationship down to one that is purely physical. Chokers effectively say to your dog, 'You pull and I will strangle you.' Use a short, webbing or leather lead and a strong, leather headcollar (*see* Chapter 4) to prevent pulling. Lead-walk training, both in urban

Even older German Shepherds such as Megan, at nine years of age, enjoy play sessions. Ball retrieval is an ideal game in that it teaches a dog to fetch and give up items, which is submissive. Brief five- to ten-minute sessions are preferable to extended periods of play.

Pre-school for young dogs: teaching basic instructions

Early in the puppy's life you can start very basic training with the doggy equivalent of pre-school. Such preliminary training will establish good habits at an early stage, which will make training the older puppy easier. Ask your vet for details of any puppy socialization and basic training classes in your area. In addition to this you can introduce your puppy to basic instructions at home. Start with simple but important word-association training.

The Stand instruction can be taught by repeating the word out loud while your puppy is standing on four paws and you are rewarding the behaviour with a treat, vocal congratulation or a stroke.

The Down instruction can easily be taught by first pointing down to the floor and then enticing your puppy to lie down by holding a treat at floor level. Once your puppy has gone down, repeat the word out loud several times while rewarding your puppy.

The Sit instruction can be introduced by holding a food treat in your raised hand (out of reach), while at the same time you use the other hand to point to your puppy's bottom. Believe it or not, your puppy will often sit as a reaction to this because of a combination of indignation, confusion and wanting to protect his bottom! Once you link the word Sit with a reward, the Sit position will quickly become associated with the action and reinforced with the reward.

The Stay instruction is probably the most difficult one to teach. It is possible to condition a puppy to stay by using Sit and then introducing Stay while a helper holds the puppy back until your instruction is made. If the puppy is rewarded with a little fuss and a treat once he has responded to your call to end the Stay, he will remember this and will usually repeat the action for the prize. It is vital that only one instruction is taught in a very short session (five minutes or so). Make sure the Sit is thoroughly established before moving on to the Stay instruction.

The Heel can be taught by offering your puppy lead-walk games from room to room around your home. Promote closeness and your puppy's attention by using a shortened lead and clicking and treating (*see* page 49) or offering food rewards combined with vocal congratulations for success.

If you wish to take your dog to training classes, ask your veterinary surgeon or search the web for a local dog trainer. It is good to ask other GSD owners if they know of any professionally organized classes. Dogs with psychological conditions (aggression and nervousness) should not be taken to training classes until behavioural treatment has been successfully undertaken.

a German Shepherd Dog needs leadership and unambiguous instructions. Clear, basic training introduced in early puppyhood will offer both.

Getting Started

Unless you happen upon the perfect puppy, training a dog requires time and plenty of patience and understanding. However, the satisfaction that can be derived when your dog learns a new command is well worth the effort.

Dogs learn mainly by association, actions or events. Immediate reward for good behaviour is therefore essential if you are to instil in your dog the motivation to obey you. The reward that most people associate with training is the food treat, but it can simply be your enthusiastic contact, physical patting and attention, vocal congratulations, and so on. If you make a fuss and congratulate when a good response is made your puppy will easily associate your instruction and his consequent action with a happy moment. Reward can also be provided by training aids (*see* page 48).

During the initial training period, keep a supply of dog treats especially for use in training sessions. Always have them ready in your pocket so that success can be signalled instantly in a positive manner.

It is important to build up trust during training and, to this end, you should never smack or shout aggressively at your puppy or dog. Do not scold him if he returns slowly or late to instructions as this will eventually promote only mistrust and poor recall instead of obedience, and can even promote aggressive or nervous behaviour. Shouting at a puppy is 'barking'. Try not to feel angry, frustrated or disappointed if a puppy fails to respond to your basic instructions: it can take a number of attempts to successfully accomplish a new task, and dogs can sense human feelings of disappointment and frustration – even when you are not shouting. Some dogs will find this demoralizing, while more dominant characters will attempt to exploit the situation and turn it into a silly game. Always signal undesirable behaviour with a sharp, low-toned 'No!' or with training discs (*see* page 53), and promote good behaviour with a food reward and vocal and physical congratulations.

Your puppy will always learn best while he is enjoying himself. For this reason daily training sessions should be kept short and enjoyable.

First Words

You can begin teaching your German Shepherd puppy to come to you or to heel to your command within the first months of his new life with you. In the house or garden, you should instruct your puppy to come after calling out his name in a confident, cheerful tone of voice. The tone is important in making your dog want to come to you. A dog will soon learn a name that is used repeatedly during interactive periods, and then you can begin simple training instructions. In the early days of training you can also use gestures such as patting your knee to visually encourage your puppy to recall to your instruction.

So, along with his name, the first words to teach a young puppy are those of basic recall: 'Come' (or 'Here'). Of course, it is not the word that the puppy understands but the sounds, which he then links with whatever actions or events are going on at the same time. If you always announce the word 'Walk' to your puppy and then handle or attach a dog lead to his collar, he will make a powerful association between the lead, going out, and the phonetic sounds 'W' and 'K'.

If a puppy refuses to recall on instruction then is it best to use distraction to obtain his attention, such as sounding an audible whistle that has already been linked to a food reward to motivate recall (*see* reward whistle, page 51). It can sometimes help to hold up a toy, or sound a squeaky toy, or rustle a treat package. A curious German Shepherd will come running if he thinks you have something interesting. If necessary, you can use an extending lead or lunge rein to create physical control at a distance. (Always use

When a dog is sitting he is in a passive position. A dog can be encouraged to respond to a Sit instruction with the promise of a food treat, a pat, or the opportunity to play.

Training rewards

Training a German Shepherd to respond quickly to instructions is best implemented if it is introduced with rewards: simple, unambiguous sounds, signals or food treats.

Day-to-day training can usually be achieved and reinforced with standard dog treats or 'complete', dry dog food. However, when developing a new training routine or technique it may be necessary to use special food rewards to focus and stimulate your puppy. More sophisticated training – establishing the use of the reward whistle to promote recall, interrupting hyperactivity towards strangers and other dogs, retrieving a specific personal item, such as a shoe or clothing – may also require special food rewards. These might be small pieces of meat, dried liver, or lightly microwaved fatty mince. In some cases, it can be worth experimenting with different types of food reward: you may find that one type is more effective than another.

Food treats are not the only type of reward available to the trainer. A reward can be anything that a dog wants and that you are able to give. Other types of reward include your attention, physical contact, a novel or squeaky toy, a ball, and so on. Do not restrict yourself to using only one type of reward for all training. Some owners and dog trainers have found that different rewards work in different situations.

Recipe for dried liver treats
450kg/1lb chopped raw liver
450kg/1lb plain flour
2 eggs
1 teaspoon garlic powder or fresh garlic
Water to moisten

Mix the ingredients together in a food-processor as for paté. Spread out the mixture in a baking tin and then cook for 30–40 minutes (or until cooked through) in an oven at 180°C (350°F/Gas mark 4). Remove from the oven and leave to cool. Once cooled, cut into small squares.

Liver treats should be used sparingly and in very small amounts as offal should not be eaten in excess. Also bear in mind that older dogs require a lower-protein diet than younger dogs. You can reduce the protein content of this recipe by replacing half the liver with potato or rice. It is always advisable to use a healthy recipe for training with treats rather than use foods such as cheese or other high-protein foods that may promote hyperactivity.

gloves to protect your hands from a rope burn as or when it is necessary to pull the dog in.)

To teach your puppy to sit on command, give him the Sit instruction in a low-toned voice and hold up your hand as if to stop traffic (sometimes offer a food treat at the same time). If you are lucky he will sit back. If your puppy appears to avoid sitting, you should say 'No', hold the treat up, and then say 'Sit' in a bright-toned voice. Sometimes a dog will sit as if to ask what is needed. Then you can congratulate your puppy and offer a food reward. He will soon get the right idea.

After about three to four months your puppy should understand most of the basic commands and will enjoy responding to them. (Older dogs that have been untrained may take longer to accept new signals.)

Social Graces

The 'love me, love my dog' attitude gives rise to the development of excitable, antisocial behaviour during the early puppy stages. It is therefore important to teach a puppy the social graces expected of him when greeting you and visitors. Jumping up, boisterous greetings, hyperactivity and suchlike might be considered amusing when displayed by a lovable puppy, but some of these amusing behaviours can become intimidating or at the very least a nuisance when displayed by an adult dog. For this reason alone it is better to teach a puppy the correct way to behave from the very beginnings of a relationship.

Teaching a dog social graces requires establishing calm behaviour that can be rewarded by you and visitors into your home. Your puppy soon learns that the sound of the doorbell or a knock on the door precedes the postman or the arrival of visitors. It may be difficult to teach your dog the ideal way to behave when surprise visitors arrive because you can be caught between the two stools of greeting them and controlling your puppy. However, when you know that a visitor is due to arrive, it is perfectly possible to start training before the event. Establish a series of recalls and sits, which can all be praised and rewarded with a food titbit. Ask your visitors to wait to enter until you are ready with your puppy recalled and in the Sit position.

Walk to the door with your puppy and continually praise any calmness. Instruct your puppy to sit again, and then open the door. The visitors should be welcomed and allowed to enter with a greeting to you, but at this stage they should ignore your puppy. Offer your puppy a food treat for being good and sitting at the door. When you, the puppy and visitors have moved to the room of your choice, instruct your puppy to sit and reward with a food treat. Now ask your visitors to offer a food treat to your puppy as a reward for sitting. If your puppy jumps up or shows signs of hyperactivity, say a firm 'No!' and avoid any direct contact by turning your back on him. Give the Sit instruction again and reward any obedience. It is also possible to use training discs (*see* pages 49 and 53) to signal non-reward for such problem behaviour.

This basic training will promote good behaviour and reduce any potential hyperactivity. Repeated events will show your puppy how to behave and react to visitors and strangers in your home. With older dogs, especially those that have been rescued or re-homed, it may be necessary to create controlled scenarios in order to change problem behaviours (*see* Chapter 6).

Hand-signals

Hand-signals can be extremely useful. They help to reinforce the verbal command by giving the dog a visual cue. But they are also invaluable when you come to start distance control exercises: if your dog understands hand-signals he will be able to respond to your instructions even when he can't quite hear you.

To teach a German Shepherd puppy hand-signals, you must use them whenever you use the basic commands. For example:

'Come'
Bring your hand towards you and pat your knee.

'Sit'
Hold your hand out with your palm facing down in front of your puppy.

'Down'
Point down to the floor.

'Move off'
Point forwards.

'Heel'
Point to your foot.

'Sit-stay'
Hold your hand out with your palm facing down in front of your puppy and point down.

'Down-stay'
Hand outstretched and gently lowered parallel to the floor.

You can create your own hand-signals providing you use them consistently.

It is vital that your puppy is socialized in every sense of the word. Once basic training has been successfully introduced and repeatedly undertaken, your puppy should be exposed to children, strangers, pets, other dogs (adults and puppies), livestock, car journeys, and anything in the house (vacuum cleaner, stereo, toaster, microwave, and so on) that may excite or disturb your puppy. During the exposure to sounds, sights and events that are triggering excitability or hyperactivity, it is important to ensure your puppy's main focus of attention is on you. Stroke your puppy and offer food treats for continued attention and good behaviour.

The use of food, attention or play rewards in the right way will help your puppy make positive associations with events that can sometimes, without care and attention to social training, lead to problem behaviours in adulthood. Puppy behavioural problems can range from play-biting to jumping up, mouthing or excessive barking. In situations where problem behaviours are being shown at an early age, offer a low-toned 'No' and turn away without giving direct attention. Eventually call your puppy to heel.

Training with Aids

Once your puppy has progressed with basic training and becomes confident and adventurous outdoors, you can introduce training aids to reinforce obedient behaviour. These aids are used in a type of psychological, or association, training now referred to as classical conditioning. This entails conditioning the animal to make a strong association between a specific sound and a natural stimulus, such as food. Research has shown that if the association between the sound and the natural stimulus is strong enough, the animal will respond to the sound signal in the same way as he does to the natural stimulus. This is because in all animals (including humans) there is a chemical reaction in the brain, or physiological response, to events or experiences. So, for example, the experience of receiving food will trigger salivation every time the animal anticipates food.

The theory behind classical conditioning was proved in the famous experiments conducted on a group of dogs by Ivan Pavlov, who showed that this natural response to the presentation of food (salivation) could be triggered by the ringing of a bell if the dog was conditioned to associate food with the ringing sound. In the experiments, he rang the bell just before presenting the dogs with food. He did this repeatedly and consistently until the dogs began to salivate at the sound of the bell, even when food was not present. The bell had therefore become what is called a positive reinforcer. The principle behind classical conditioning can also be used in the opposite way. An association can be made between a particular sound and something that the dog wishes to avoid (such as the removal of food or the withdrawal of attention); this sound is then known as a negative reinforcer.

Reinforcement using sound is especially useful in training dogs because of the canine's highly developed and well-tuned sense of hearing. Such reinforcement takes place all the time, often without our being aware of it. For example, many dog owners marvel at their dog's ability to tell the difference between the sound of the dog-food container being opened and that of any number of other similar containers being opened. The same might be said of footsteps belonging to the postman as he comes up the path and those of a family member.

The dog's ability to make such precise associations is extremely useful to animal trainers because once you have established an association between a specific sound and an event, the effect is greater and longer lasting than most other methods of training. There are other advantages. It is immediate and accurate: the sound made by a training aid can be delivered at the instant the animal displays a behaviour, so the animal knows precisely what action is being praised (or discouraged); a food treat or vocal praise takes longer to deliver, by which time the animal may be thinking about something else. The

Training aids: essential facts and rules

The three training aids referred to in this book have the following basic uses or meanings.

Clicker: *reward*.
Signals 'Yes' to good behavioiur.

Reward whistle: *interruption*.
For recall and interrupting problem behaviours.

Training discs: *non-reward*
Signals 'No' to undesirable behaviour.

Before they can be effective, all the training aids must be linked to something else in the dog's brain: the clicker and reward whistle must be associated with reward; the training discs must be associated with the withdrawal of reward. Once the link is made, the sound of the aid will on its own represent reward (or non-reward) – although in order to maintain the conditioning long term you should occasionally give food treats (or, in the case of the discs, withdraw them) to reinforce the association with the training aid.

Clicker
- Most young dogs will eventually become addicted to the simple sound-reward system.
- Noise-sensitive dogs should always be introduced to clicker training outdoors.
- When the clicker signal is established, its use triggers dopamine (anticipation) and serotonin (reward) in the dog's brain. It mentally stimulates your dog.
- It is vital that the clicker is sounded only as and during the moment he responds to your instruction.
- Clicked at the wrong time, the device can inadvertently signal reward for inappropriate behaviour.
- You do not need to point the clicker at your dog. It is the sound and its associated

reward that become programmed into the subconscious.

Reward whistle
- Noise-sensitive dogs should always be introduced to whistle training outdoors.
- It is vital that the whistle sound-signals are used randomly during the initial exposure so that a puppy does not associate them with a particular event (such as feeding, excessive barking, the presence of a stranger, child, other dog, or moving target). You can then use the whistle to interrupt behaviours.
- It is advisable to repeat random sessions within your home. Stand in another room to your puppy, sound the whistle and reward obedience (recall and sit) with either a food treat or a pat and vocal congratulation or a two-minute retrieval play session.

Training discs
- It is important to repeatedly use the training discs *only when* the behaviour is being shown. Post-event signalling will only confuse a dog and will reduce the effectiveness of the signalling. Even if your dog appears contrite after committing a misdemeanour (such as inappropriate urination), it is not effective to use the training discs after the event.
- The sooner the training discs are used as the particular behaviour is shown the better. If a dog is allowed to become extremely hyperactive before they are used, the effectiveness of the training discs will be diminished.
- The discs should not be used to scare a puppy or dog.
- Your dog should never have physical contact with the discs. Always hold on to the discs during training, or keep them close to you so that you can intercept if there is a possibility that your dog will pick them up.

training aid is also consistent: the sound it makes does not depend on a particular person's voice or tone – so all family members can use it with equal authority as the signal and reinforcement for good behaviour – and it is not affected by the handler's mood.

The Clicker
A clicker is a thumb-sized plastic unit with a thin metal film that, when pressed, sends out a distinctive 'click-click' sound. It is a speedy, non-vocal, positive reinforcer that communicates with your puppy or dog to promote

Clicker training can be introduced during play sessions. The promise of a chance to play a ball-retrieval game can be used to promote and signal (with a click and a food treat) an obedient response. Here, Max has given Sit and Wait instructions before throwing the ball.

Although the clicker is initially always associated with a food treat, the reward can eventually be varied: a stroke, verbal congratulations, or a toy being used to promote good behaviour. However, in the long term it is important that food treats continue to be used occasionally to prevent the loss of the clicker's association with food.

appropriate or good behaviour. The unique clicker sound, when exclusively linked to a food reward, eventually signals reward alone, without the need for additional reinforcement (attention, pats, vocal congratulations, and so on). In other words, as with Pavlov's dogs, the clicker signal becomes the 'reward' in itself because, once conditioned, a dog's brain will not be able to separate the food-treat reward from the sound that has become strongly associated with it. New research has shown that the area in the brain that responds to reward also deals with addiction and compulsion, which may explain why animals take to this advanced, but simple, training so quickly.

It may take a few attempts to begin conditioning your puppy or dog to associate the sound of the clicker with reward, but it rarely takes more than a day or so. Initially, the reward associated with the clicker signal should be food-based – dog biscuits, liver treats (*see* recipe on page 46), small pieces of meat – but eventually it can be a pat or a vocal congratulation, 'Good dog!' or similar. As with all the training aids, however, occasional return to the use of a food treat is necessary to maintain the conditioning.

The clicker should be used whenever your puppy or dog correctly responds to an instruction. The clicker does not need to be pointed at a dog, and it should be sounded *only* as he responds to your command. This is essential: any delay will confuse your dog and render the clicker as inaccurate as your voice or the delivery of a food treat.

Introducing the clicker
The early steps to teaching and conditioning your puppy or dog to understand what the clicker means requires a brief session where they are first introduced:

1. Have the clicker and some 'smelly' food treats ready.

2. Call your puppy to you from a distance, and instruct him to sit.

3. As he obeys, click, and then give the food treat and copious praise.

4. Repeat the procedure several times. Eventually, your puppy or dog will begin to focus his attention on the clicker in anticipation of the treat.

The clicker can be used in a variety of situations in which your dog displays behaviour that you wish to encourage (responding to instructions, calmness, and so on). Whenever your dog displays the desired behaviour, click, treat and praise him.

Reward Whistle
The reward whistle works on a similar principle to the clicker in that it is linked to a significant treat. However, it has the advantage of being clearly audible when you are not close by your dog, so it can be used to promote recall at a distance on walks or around the home. This is especially useful for dogs that display selective hearing: some dogs continue following a scent or chasing after other dogs apparently oblivious to the owner's instruction to return.

As with the clicker, the whistle must be linked to a reward in order to motivate your dog to respond. All good responses to the whistle should be signalled with a 'click' and reinforced with an appropriate dog treat (not chocolate or cheese because these foods may encourage hyperactivity and can be detrimental to your dog's health).

The reward whistle can be introduced in much the same way as the clicker. Sound the whistle and recall your dog; instruct him to sit, and then click and reward. It is important that during the initial introduction it is used randomly (calling your dog from the garden or another room), otherwise he may

Ruth, shown here with Remy, is preparing to throw a ball for retrieval. She has the reward whistle ready to sound in order to promote a speedy recall.

Now that the ball has been successfully retrieved and willingly given up, Ruth begins to repeat the training sequence by instructing Remy to adopt the Down position. As Remy has responded correctly, Ruth is preparing to throw the ball again as a reward.

You can tackle a specific problem behaviour (such as jumping up, excessive barking, and so on) in a special training session in which you wait for the problem behaviour to be displayed and then sound the training discs at the same time as showing a food treat and removing it. The dog learns by association that the sound of the discs means a reward is not being given, and this can be associated with the problem behaviour being shown at the time.

associate the whistle with a particular event (such as the arrival of a family member, visitor, another dog, the postman, and so on).

Training Discs

Training discs comprise five 50mm (2in) brass discs, which are held together on a handy cord and make a very distinctive sound when shaken and dangled or dropped on the ground. They produce a signal that is the exact opposite to the clicker sound in that it is associated with the *removal* of a food or toy reward. The discs therefore act as a negative reinforcer. Once association is established they can be used to signal that you wish a particular behaviour to cease. As with the other training aids, the sound of the discs becomes embedded in your dog's subconscious. They are especially useful for rescue, re-homed and older dogs that have not been exposed to training.

Once your puppy or dog has been conditioned to understand that the sound of the discs represents the removal of a reward (the opposite to the clicker) they can be used to

deal with many problem behaviours such as rushing through doors, excessive barking, attention-seeking, jumping up, growling, and so on.

Introducing training discs

The steps to teaching and conditioning your puppy or dog to understand what the training discs mean are a little more lengthy, and require a bit more time and patience, than the introduction of the clicker requires. Once again, the aid should be introduced in brief sessions:

1. Have the training discs and some 'smelly' food treats ready.

2. Call your puppy to you from a distance, instruct him to sit, and give him a food treat from your hand.

3. Place another treat on the floor between your feet (with small to medium-sized dogs this is best done when you are seated), and move your hand away.

Ruth shows Remy the training discs during a special introductory session.

can invent another command specifically associated with the training discs. This word should contain a strong consonant. A client had real success calling the training discs 'jangles', and when announced as a threat ('Where are the jangles?'), the dog ceased hyperactive behaviour.

Do not give your dog any other attention apart from the signal. If your dog stops the particular unwanted behaviour prepare to announce a bright 'Yes', or use the clicker and a food treat to reward obedience once your dog is in the Sit position.

Training discs prove the most successful when used long term. However, the most important thing is that they are used consistently and with good timing: never use training discs to signal failure after the event. To maintain their association with non-reward, repeat the set-up session on a monthly basis.

4. As the dog attempts to take the treat, quickly exchange it for the discs. Place the treat in your pocket. (This needs to be a single, fast action, so before you start it is a good idea to practise doing it without your dog.) The discs need only to be sounded. They should not be thrown or rattled excessively.

5. Repeat the procedure several times. Eventually, your puppy or dog will sit down or withdraw, and will cease attempts to take the treat.

Using training discs
The training discs can be used in a variety of situations in which your dog displays any behaviour that you would like to eliminate (such as jumping up, hyperactivity, excessive barking, targeting moving cars or people, running through doorways first, and so on). Whenever your dog displays such behaviour, sound the training discs, show your dog the food/treat in your hand, say 'No', and then turn away. Rather than use the word No, you

Lead-training

When your puppy is about 12 weeks old, you will be able to begin teaching him how to walk to your heel on a lead. Outside of the home or garden it is essential to keep your puppy on a close lead, i.e., a short lead that will maintain a puppy close to your side. This will not only 'transmit' your control and confidence but it will prevent your puppy from leaping about or being distracted. Lead-training in both urban and rural settings, once your puppy has been inoculated against diseases, is essential and should always be accompanied by food rewards for good behaviour following instructions such as Stop, Sit and Wait. If your dog is nervous near roads, people or other dogs, instruct him to sit, then click and reward with a pat, treat and/or vocal congratulation. This will reinforce your leadership, which will in turn inspire your dog's trust and confidence.

While walking, try to maintain your puppy close to your side and frequently use the com-

When heel-walking your dog, it is important to use a strong, short lead to maintain the dog close to your side.

The headcollar is similar to the bridle and reins used to control horses in that the means of control (in this case the lead) is attached to the side of the head. If your dog pulls, his head will be turned sideways, making it impossible for him to lean against the collar and pull.

mand 'Heel'. If your puppy always pulls to go ahead (often mistaken for enthusiasm), stop and instruct your puppy to heel in a firm, clear, low-toned voice, drawing your pet nearer to your side. Once your puppy successfully responds, announce the Sit instruction and continue only when there is a response. This method will signal that pulling behaviour is unacceptable and that your puppy is required to accept your control.

It is better not to use a full, or even half, choke/check-chain as these rather primitive aids allow a dog to exert a physical challenge during walks. To prevent pulling, head-control collars are ideal because they prevent the dog from 'leaning' on the collar, which pulling dogs rely on to forge their way forward. The headcollar exerts control to the side of the head, so, if your dog pulls, his head is automatically turned sideways. This

is essential because a dog will not go forward if he cannot look in the direction he is going. These 'Dogmatic' headcollars have proved very successful with clients in my clinic. They are enough to promote control if you have trained your puppy correctly from the outset, and have proved better than body harnesses and other similar devices.

Control Walks

As a healthy German Shepherd puppy grows he will become physically stronger. At this stage it is essential that psychological

During a Control Walk, the dog is instructed to sit at various predetermined points. Obedience is signalled with the clicker (above) *and rewarded* (right).

Once a dog has been rewarded for a Stop, Sit and Wait, he should be instructed to walk on. Obedience to each instruction should be clicked and rewarded.

control is in force and is consistently maintained. A dog needs to look up to his owner, and it is therefore important that you play the role of 'pack leader'. Showing that you, as the owner and pack leader, are 'in charge' is not about physically restraining your dog. It is always better to have psychological restraint in an intensive training session to promote control.

One of the most effective ways of doing this is through my specially developed training stroll, which I call the 'Control Walk' because of its repeated Stop, Sit, Wait, and Walk-on instructive-style. A Control Walk requires you to undertake a ten minutes' stroll, ideally on a daily basis, whilst giving repeated instructions at various landmarks. The Control Walk will offer your dog a concentrated training session with reward for good behaviour, and the close lead-work will become a means to communicate your leadership qualities. One of the great advantages of Control Walks is that any family member or friend can undertake them.

Ideally a Control Walk should be given on a daily basis together with at least one daily freestyle walk. Control Walk sessions must be signalled and rewarded (with clicker, treats and vocal congratulations) to positively reinforce the instructions. The walk is successful in focusing your dog on your leadership and, when accepted, into seeking your guidance and instructions.

Control Walk Procedure

It is important to have lead, shoes, coats and keys ready in advance to reduce delays that can act as cues for hyperactivity or frustration in your dog. Use a short lead and collar that maintains your dog close to your side.

Choose between five and ten roadside landmarks near to home. These landmarks (lamp posts, gateways, kerbsides, and so on) should be about 25m (or yards) apart. Once you have decided the route and the landmarks you can begin.

1. Approach the door or gate and instruct your dog to sit. Slightly open the door or gate. If your dog anticipates and attempts to squeeze through, firmly shut the door or gate in front of both of you. Give the Sit instruction and repeat until the dog realizes that the only way for him to pass the threshold is to do it on your instruction.

   This first step is very important because a challenging dog will want to go before you. This is not simply youthful anticipation but an expression of the pack- or team-leader's right to go ahead of the rest. Overcoming this first hurdle will help set the ground rules for the rest of the Control Walk.

2. Make your way to the first landmark. Halt your dog firmly about a metre away from it. Using a low-toned voice, instruct your dog to sit, then click, treat and praise obedience.

Control Walk: Dos and Don'ts

Do:
- Have all equipment and paraphernalia such as your keys ready in advance so that there are no delays in leaving for the walk.
- Walk your dog on a short, leather or nylon strap lead attached to his standard collar that will maintain your pet near to your side. Headcollars, when side-fastened, are excellent for control.
- Click and reward all obedience shown, especially in the early days.
- If possible, vary the walk direction each day.
- Ask family members and friends to Control-walk your dog.
- Speak in a clear but low-toned voice to communicate your dominance.

Do not:
- Shout any instructions (shouting is literally barking at your dog).
- Walk on or proceed to the next instruction until your dog has obeyed each instruction. This is vital in preventing leadership challenges.
- Use a choke/check-chain.
- Allow your dog to precede you through gates or other thresholds.

---

3. When you are ready (and only then), instruct your dog to move on. Say 'Go', 'Walk on', 'Move on', or 'OK' – it can be any command that you have decided to use as long as you use it consistently. If your dog pulls, immediately instruct him to sit. Do not proceed to the next instruction until your dog has responded obediently.

4. When you have completed the route, return to the place within your house where the walk began. Give the final Sit instruction, and dismiss your dog.

Throughout the walk, click and treat each instruction that is obeyed. It is vital that you

This sequence of pictures clearly illustrates a German Shepherd Dog that does not want to accept his owner as leader. The dog is not concentrating on his owner, and his body language reveals a lack of interest in her directional guidance and instructions. It is important that the owner does not exacerbate the problem by moving to the next instruction before the first one has been obeyed, as this will reinforce the dog's perception that he need not co-operate.

do not shout out any instructions. To a dog, a shouting voice represents barking and this will cause anxiety in your dog. If a dog should ignore any given instructions, show a food treat but do not give it up until the particular instruction has been obeyed.

If possible, vary the walk direction each day so that your dog does not come to anticipate the route and its landmarks. Once your dog is following your instructions and begins to stop, sit and stay in anticipation, halve the number of Stop and Sit points.

It is a good idea to ask family members and friends to Control-walk your dog. They and older children can play a vital role in that they can also communicate control to your dog and reinforce the 'bottom of the pack' status to him while promoting the higher pack status of the young handler.

Freestyle Walks

In contrast to the Control Walk, freestyle or off-lead walks simply allow your dog to run off some energy. They also mean he can dictate some important controlling aspects of interaction. However, even during freestyle walks, it is possible to exercise distance-control training by developing food-rewarded recall linked to a reward-whistle signal and occasionally offering the reward of a short interactive play session.

For most domesticated dogs, walks probably represent and replace the hunting and foraging expeditions that would naturally occur in the wild. Some nervous dogs are less than enthusiastic about walks – perhaps even refusing them because they cannot 'control' these events – but the majority of dogs would enjoy as many walks as an owner could fit into each day until all those taking part succumbed to exhaustion! Most become acutely excited by the prospect of a walk and often respond immediately to visual and sound cues (changing shoes, coats, picking up keys, and so on). To promote calm behaviour, reduce any obvious stimuli and generally make less 'fuss' prior to walks.

Walk times are an ideal time for developing the bond between you and your dog. However, it is important to have complete control of him when out in public places. He should be allowed freestyle walks only when you are confident that a recall instruction will always be 100 per cent successful.

It is normal for your dog to explore and become excited during walks. However, general walks can become more controlled with the following preparation:

At home, during a short session in the garden, sound the reward whistle, recall your dog, and offer a click/food reward for sitting by your side. Repeat five or six times. Follow this sequence, once it has proved successful, with the retrieval of a favourite toy (frisbees, balls or dumb-bells are best) or bone. This training should prove beneficial during freestyle walks. Phase out the food reward over the weeks by occasionally replacing it with vocal congratulations and a pat.

To combat recall problems during walks, the random use of the reward whistle is essential. If your dog is recalled only during 'exciting events' (the arrival of other dogs, strangers, and so on) then this association will be made and the problem behaviour will increase. The usual freestyle walks taken with your dog may still be enjoyed during any necessary training or retraining, but they are best restricted, and owner control should be exercised at all times. Using a new route in an unfamiliar area will often encourage a dog to be more responsive to recall signals.

When retraining, if there are problem behaviours being shown towards other dogs or strangers, it may be better to prevent your dog from confronting strangers by retraining him with an extending lead or lunge-line. It is important not to make any event of aggression or disobedience during training or walks exciting by offering your dog excessive attention as this will only turn the event into a game and will encourage problem behaviours. Always finish a training session on a positive note with a well-rewarded click-and-treat Control Walk or brief retrieval session with a ball.

If your dog exhibits aggressive or excitable modes of behaviour during walks (i.e., tail out, hair standing up, lungeing, pulling, barking, growling) use distraction: show your dog a novel toy or sound a whistle or novel squeaky toy, call your dog to your side and, on arrival, instruct him to sit. Immediately offer him a click and a significant food reward. If a dog is not treat-orientated, use a novel toy as a device to hold his attention.

Brief play/retrieval interactions can take place on freestyle walks. These should last no more than five minutes. It is better to have several bursts of play than to have one, long session. This will help to prevent hyperactivity and promote your control of the situation. Dictate the retrieval item to be used, and instigate and cease the game after each mini play session during the walk.

Training Games

Retrieval

The roots of canine play lie in the development of instinctive challenging behaviour amongst young dogs and wolves in nature. The wild siblings will compete over pieces of the kill such as clean bones or skin, and these items are used to continually test each other's strength and resolve. In domestication, the 'bones' to be challenged over are a dog's toys and chews, and various items belonging to humans. For this reason, the

Once a toy has been retrieved, your dog should be clearly instructed to sit. He should then immediately give up the toy.

most important training for powerful working dog breeds revolves around retrieval games, which are best undertaken as early as possible within the home, back yard or garden. Outdoor retrieval games, which should last no longer than five to ten minutes, can be developed with a ball or frisbee.

Retrieval games reinforce an owner's pack leadership because they require a dog to be submissive. This does not mean that a dog will not enjoy them, especially when success is rewarded with a food treat and congratulation. With some effort and patience an owner can quickly teach a dog to chase and retrieve a ball, dumb-bell or toy bone, recall, give, and then sit for a reward. Click and treat all successful retrievals. The reward can also be

a pat, a vocal congratulation or a treat, or initially a combination of all three.

Your dog may not respond immediately, but always persevere and praise success. A testing dog – one that is often described in canine literature as dominant – will not want to give up the retrieved toy. He may dance around you and display head-turning behaviour in an attempt to encourage you into a challenging game. This type of German Shepherd personality will want an owner to wrestle a toy free in order to turn the game into a challenge, but it is undoubtedly a mistake to be drawn into this game. Avoid the physical challenge because an adult GSD will eventually turn this into disobedience or even aggression. A happy dog will usually give up a toy for a food treat or for another toy that the owner has in his possession.

The sight of a food reward can encourage a challenging pet to give up the toy that he has brought back. Or you can offer another toy, and the dog will usually give up the one that he is carrying and attempt to access the one being held. It is advisable to use the clicker system to signal that giving up an item that has been retrieved is the correct behaviour, and then it is possible to promote the perfect retrieval by clicking and rewarding a dog for placing the toy in the hand.

Search and Foraging Games

Search and foraging games are an ideal way to stimulate a German Shepherd Dog mentally and to develop positive behaviour towards food and toy retrieval.

It is always easier to work with dogs on an individual basis. However, if several dogs are involved, or an owner frequently walks with other dogs (belonging to friends or family) that are sociable with each other, it may be possible to encourage 'group' hunting and foraging games. However, this should be abandoned if there is any sign of aggression and/or excessive competitiveness.

Dougal is at his happiest as Andrew launches the frisbee in the retrieval game. It is important to make retrieval games brief – and rewarded – to promote obedience and your control, and to prevent hyperactivity.

Dougal returns with the frisbee and sits, awaiting the next instruction from Andrew.

Andrew offers the food reward in exchange for the successfully retrieved (and submissively released) frisbee.

The food-foraging game

In nature, at least 50 per cent of a dog's time is devoted to group hunting and foraging or the search of prey food. In domestication, food is placed in a dish on the floor and that's it! In human terms, this is the equivalent of being prevented from achieving any objectives through work or study.

To combat this you can use food to challenge your dog's intelligence. Instead of simply offering your dog food in a dish, organize hide-and-seek games with the usual food ration split into equal portions.

To begin with, the foraging area should be confined to an appropriate area within your home and garden, and your dog should be allowed visual contact with the area so that he can learn the object of the game. Place measured amounts of food into open or semi-sealed tubs or packets (but nothing too difficult to open). Hide half or all of your

Healthy German Shepherds thrive on the enjoyment of a retrieval session. Dougal expresses his enthusiasm with a burst of energy and exuberance.

dog's normal food rations. For the first game it is advisable to make at least one of the portions fairly easy to locate and the food easy to access. In subsequent games it may be possible to make the access and location increasingly difficult. Hide a dish behind a garden plant pot and another under a plastic container. Try to imagine how his scent location works, and use interesting variations to attract your dog into searching.

When you are ready, release the dog at the door threshold from where the seek and locate game can commence. Say 'Yes', or 'Find' – or whatever command you have decided to use for the game – in a bright tone. Encourage him to search and find the food locations. If the dog searches in the wrong places, say 'No' very firmly. However, be ready to congratulate and praise (use the reward whistle if necessary) when each cache of food has been located.

Eventually, the foraging game can be as complicated as the intelligence of a German Shepherd puppy allows. The number of food portions can be increased and the location difficulty can also be developed.

Search and selection games
Search and selection games are an excellent and mutually satisfying way of using your dog's mental, rather than his physical, abilities. The games require the use of different toys or cloth items.

For the selection game, the items are placed or thrown a distance away. The dog is then sent to fetch a particular one. The preliminary to this is to introduce a simple interactive game to encourage mental ability: the 'Yes and No' game. This is a short, five-minute game using different toys, such as a training dummy, a ball or frisbee, in which you teach the dog to associate a particular toy with its name. To make the learning process easier, select two toys and smear one (the one you want him to select) with a

liver treat. Say the name of this toy, especially emphasizing the consonant sound. If your dog sniffs this toy, announce his success with a bright 'Yes!' and a click. If he picks up the toy, sound the reward whistle and reward his recall and offering up of the toy with a food treat and a congratulatory fuss. Say a dull 'No' if he sniffs the wrong one.

Initially, the game should be based on two items, but eventually it can involve as many items as your dog's instinct or intelligence allows. Proceed as follows:

1. Set out the items to be selected.

2. Have your dog on the lead or in the Sit and Stay position.

3. Release your dog from his lead, or end the Stay instruction with 'OK', and tell your dog the name of the item that has to be retrieved. Then instruct him to select it by announcing an action word such as 'Fetch' or 'Bring' (whatever command you use for this).

4. Say 'Yes' brightly when he selects the correct item, and click and treat when he brings it back. If the incorrect one is selected and returned, say 'No' (gently) and send him out again. This encourages your dog to make a selection on your instructions rather than on his whims.

In the early stages it is possible to make the selection game easier by marking the required item with your scent or with a treat.

A far simpler game involves the scent-location of a hidden toy. This game can be played in the home, in the garden or back yard, or on walks. First scent the item using a liver treat or your own scent (armpits are great for this!) and then hide it behind the settee, under a bush or plastic plant pot, or in the long grass. While you do this your dog should be instructed to stay in another room, or, on a walk, he should be held back by your partner or other family member. You can then release him to search and find. The clicker can be used to signal success and the reward whistle can signal that a recall and return with the item will result in a big fuss and a special food treat. To an intelligent breed, like a German Shepherd, this game is better than your night out on the town.

Benefits of Training

A German Shepherd that is both trained to instructions and mentally stimulated will repay his owner every day with obedience and faithfulness. This dog will be happy and willing to please because he knows your leadership qualities and will be content to allow you to control the relationship.

This breed is both mentally and physically strong and will quickly seize an opportunity to dictate terms to a submissive owner. This is not antisocial behaviour – as we would know it in human terms – but rather an instinct-driven attempt to move up the pecking order. With some German Shepherd personalities the owner will always have to be strong willed and, psychologically, one step ahead. Others are naturally passive and will fall into a pattern of behaviour that requires little exertion of owner control. Both types of personality benefit from training and mental challenges.

Whichever type of dog you own it is possible, by following the guidelines in this chapter, to ethically and responsibly maintain control while giving your German Shepherd a positive and rewarding lifestyle. This is the basis for a wonderful relationship.

5 Re-homing a German Shepherd

Even if you acquire a re-homed or rescue German Shepherd as a puppy, there are usually important differences between this young animal and a puppy that has had a more straightforward start in life. Re-homed puppies will undoubtedly have experienced inconsistencies and changes in environment and handling. At best, rescue dogs will be slightly disturbed by the sudden changes they must endure; at worst they may have experienced trauma and abuse. Bringing an adult German Shepherd home, and understanding the needs of a potentially traumatized dog, requires sensitivity and experience as well that extra TLC.

Many people consider adopting an adult dog because they subscribe to the idea that there are fewer house-training and chewing problems with an older German Shepherd Dog or GSD-cross than there are with a puppy. However, just the opposite can be true if a dog has had a difficult past or if a nervous adult dog is not handled correctly in the first few weeks of adoption. The very nature of a German Shepherd means that fear-based or nervous aggression may be shown in moments of confusion.

Reasons for Re-homing

It might be argued that there are as many reasons for dogs being homeless as there are dogs in rescue centres. However, these reasons tend to fall into the few basic categories that follow here.

Change in Circumstances

The previous owner may have discovered that, because of unforeseen changes in personal circumstances, such as babies being born or a move abroad, they are no longer able to care for a dog that was once the family pet. Elderly people may have gradually found themselves too infirm to look after their pets, or they may have been placed into a nursing home or a care centre that does not allow pets. This is a very distressing situation for all concerned.

Lack of Foresight/Loss of Interest

Canines in care may simply have become uncontrollable and too difficult to look after. Owners who fail to appreciate the needs of a large, intelligent working breed can find themselves out of their depth when their untrained puppy, who wasn't too much trouble as a youngster, grows into an unmanageable adult that is difficult to control: they find themselves unable to cope with the powerful and demanding adult version. Such dogs then become a liability, causing stress to their owners as well as a menace to the public.

Some people discover that they unwisely selected an unsuitable breed of dog for their lifestyle. Large and extremely active individuals require either largish homes and, ideally, a

These puppies are bright and healthy, but puppies from a rescue litter may not have had such a good start. Good socialization and adequate health care may have been lacking – laying down problems for the future.

rural environment, or a very attentive owner who is able to provide the necessary exercise and stimulation that the breed requires.

Another type of owner who also falls into this category is the one who discovers that the adorable puppy, once a great attraction to everyone in the family (especially to the children), now has much less appeal. This pet has become rather big, it smells, it costs a lot to feed, it makes a mess in the garden, it puts dirty paw-prints across the carpet, and it chews the furniture. And who wants the inconvenience of having to take the nuisance dog for a walk in the pouring rain – or even in good weather for that matter?

Failure to Fulfil Potential

Show dogs
Some breeders hold on to an individual puppy with the idea of showing him at a later stage. Sometimes the promise of a 'show-winning puppy' turns out to be what breeders call 'pet quality'. This term is not as derogatory as it may sound. All it means is that the puppy isn't quite perfect in breed standard terms. Such imperfections may take the form of the most minor defects, such as inferior (but not faulty) dentition, a muzzle that is a little too pointed, or hindquarters that are not angulated to the precise degree laid down in the breed standard. Any such small physical deficiencies that have no effect on the animal's temperament or his overall health are of no consequence to anyone outside the show ring, and such dogs can make perfectly good companions. The problem comes when a puppy that has been sold as 'show quality' is returned, within a few weeks, to the breeder by a disgruntled owner who considers that the puppy has no show potential. Such an animal may then be sold on to another owner. In cases where this happens more than once the puppy can develop many behavioural problems simply from all the confusion the repeated re-homing creates.

Dogs trained for the services
After initial training for use by the police, prison serves, armed forces or security organizations, some German Shepherd Dogs fail to make the grade. These dogs are then rejected and sometimes become available to the general public.

Finding a Dog to Adopt

Some dogs are re-homed privately in that they are passed directly from one home to another – often from the owner to a friend of a friend. These dogs are usually re-homed because of the owner's change of circumstance. Where such reasons are genuine, the dog may have been well-socialized and cared for, and the new owner should be able to obtain details about the dog's past.

The professional breeder's re-homed dog may also carry background information but it can be the most challenging of all pets. The dog may not have lived in a 'home' with a family. Most of his young life may have been spent in outdoor kennels or runs, and this factor has to be considered. Some puppies quickly adapt to a new lifestyle after re-homing, but others fail to come to terms with changes.

Any dog that has undergone or experienced guard-dog training and then been rejected should be considered as a potential companion pet only with extreme caution. A dog whose instinctive aggression behaviours have been stimulated and reinforced can be very difficult to recondition. He is much more likely to display territorial, possessive, protective and predatory aggressive behaviours, which are then exacerbated by the stress of re-homing. Such dogs often prove completely unsuitable as companion animals, and only the most resilient and dedicated dog trainer should ever consider re-homing one.

Rescue Centres

Dogs are arriving every day at animal sanctuaries or at rescue centres that specialize in a particular breed. There is often a predominance of German Shepherd Dog, retriever and Border Collie crossbreeds, and this may be because the so-called intelligent breeds are more demanding and troublesome than others, especially when they are nervous.

A rescue centre for dogs must be the closest canine equivalent of our psychiatric hospitals. I know the major organizations and those wonderful individuals who help to re-home dogs will not thank me for that comparison. However, imagine, if you can, the typical rescue centre from a dog's point of view. When your world is at least 50 per cent scent-sensed, and you are a sociable pack animal with highly developed powers of

German Shepherds that undergo training with the police or armed services will have been taught to display aggression.

hearing, it must be dreadful to 'smell' the panic, distress and the urine and faeces of dogs that you don't know, and to be surrounded by constant noise and pandemonium. Every dog will bark, some will howl and others will whine – every time a kennel attendant walks down the line, every time a visitor comes to look for a pet, and every time a new inmate is placed into a kennel that has only just been vacated by another animal. With all the kindness in the world, this environment must disturb all but the most robust and happy of dogs.

If you are rescuing a dog from this environment, it is wise to expect some emotional scars. Some dogs survive the trauma and positively respond to a new home and owner. Others find it difficult to adapt to changes and are neurotic unless behavioural therapy is undertaken. Some dogs are rescued and re-homed a number of times in their lives. Then, the level of confusion and uncertainty is raised every time.

Breed specialist rescue
A breed-specific re-homing organization or a small-scale rescue centre is usually run by dedicated individuals who often have an excellent working knowledge of the breed they represent. They will try to establish why the existing owner needs to re-home a dog, and they will almost certainly attempt to match a particular dog personality with potential owners. However, even specialist centres can have problems obtaining adequate information about an unwanted dog or batch of puppies or young dogs.

Strays

Stray dogs often end up in rescue centres, but there are occasions when dogs are 'rescued' or taken into care directly from the street by a caring person. Whilst an impulse or kindness style of rescue is commendable in many ways it can be potentially disastrous. The trauma of being a lost stray fending for himself, and being wet and cold and hungry on the streets, can take its toll on the mental state of even the brightest dogs. The dog may be relieved to find a human that offers shelter and kindness, but he is also likely to be completely disorientated and in a confused state. Be extremely wary, and do not confine the dog with anyone who might be apprehensive or frightened, especially younger children.

If you happen upon a dog that appears to be a stray, it is important that the authorities are informed and that the dog is examined by a veterinary surgeon. If the dog is unclaimed

and settles quickly into your home then the future could be bright for both parties.

In the best case scenario, a dog may have slipped free of home and eventually found himself miles away. Once lost and disorientated, and without any hope of finding his way back to safety, the dog becomes hungry and distressed. If he is reported straying, he may find himself reunited with his owners. Not so in the worst-case scenario, when the dog has been abandoned or rejected and may have been badly handled or even mistreated.

The Unknown Past

It is rare for a German Shepherd or crossbreed from a rescue centre to be accompanied by a complete background history file. Often these young and adult dogs or puppies have strayed or been abandoned, and they may even have been rehoused on several occasions. Multiple ownership of a dog can hide a dark past. Sometimes there is obvious physical evidence of mistreatment or of faulty learning (*see* Chapter 3) when the dog is first brought into the rescue centre. However, the psychological evidence of mistreatment may truly be exhibited only when the dog is transferred from the rescue centre and introduced into a new home. It may take several weeks, or even months in the most acute cases, for a rescue dog to reveal his true personality.

A dog that is found as a stray on the streets is likely to have suffered food deprivation, extreme weathers, aggression from other dogs as well as some humans. These factors force a dog to rely on his instincts, and it is no wonder that they sometimes show fear, territorial and possessive forms of aggression. It is extremely important to take these factors into account. A rescue dog needs time to recover both physically and mentally. This is more than the first week or two. Imagine a foster child that has suffered a difficult life. Dogs are not as complex as children, but they cannot be counselled in the English language or stroked better.

It is not just adult dogs that come with an unknown past and 'baggage'. An abandoned litter of puppies can pose just as many questions. What was the age and physical condition of the litter mother? How old are the puppies (sometimes difficult to gauge when they are undernourished)? How did the mating come about, and which breeds of dog were involved? What, if any, socialization has been experienced? These issues can dictate the personality of a rescue puppy.

However kind and thoughtful new owners may show themselves to be, the re-homed dog is, more often than not, disorientated, fearful and insecure. This extremely confused and stressful state may give rise to antisocial and faulty behavioural patterns that include excessive barking, hyperactivity, aggressiveness, destructiveness, and anxiety. These behaviours can also include other undesirable reactions such as inappropriate urination and defecation. In some cases, a dog may not have been properly housetrained, or he could have been confined in restricted places for extended periods.

While breed specialist rescue organizations will generally try to provide some knowledge of a dog's previous history, it is not unusual for previous owners to 'forget' to mention the antisocial side of a dog's personality, fearing that the organization or person will refuse to accept the dog. This may include extremely difficult problems such as howling and barking when left alone in the home, destructive behaviour, or inappropriate urination and defecation in the home.

Some information on a rescue or re-homed dog, it has to be said, is better than none at all. In the absence of early socialization and handling information it is possible only to guess at why a rescued dog is confused. Without knowing the past history of

---

Abused dogs

A German Shepherd Dog that has been exposed to abuse can be considered for re-homing only by expert dog handlers. Such dogs carry very negative associations with the gender and type of people and other dogs that have caused their distress. A badly treated dog will flinch at the raising of a hand even when it is to offer a pat or greeting. The abused dog will often hide away from strangers in the home or display nervous aggression. As with trained guard dogs, badly treated German Shepherds are much more likely to display fear, territorial, possessive, protective and predatory aggressive behaviours. These dogs, sadly, often then develop strong attachments to individuals who show them kindness. This type of attachment can lead to over-dependency and possessiveness.

It is possible to rehabilitate the most badly treated of dogs, but the amount of time and patience required (often between 12 and 24 months of careful handling) should be fully appreciated and planned for before deciding to take on a badly treated dog. I would advise only those that can afford behavioural treatment from an expert, or the most experienced and committed dog handlers, to consider taking on a rescue GSD.

---

an adult dog it is difficult to identify the potentially traumatic events may have caused undesirable or neurotic behaviour. A dog that flinches to a raised arm is probably easily identified as one that has been physically abused. A dog that urinates on furniture, carpets or bedding may also have been mistreated, but in a less physical way. It is wrong to attempt to deal with a dog's behavioural problems by continual acts of kindness. If a rescued animal has suffered under the care of previous handlers, and then it is suddenly swamped with kindness and attention, the result can be other problems: confusion, insecurity, or an unsettled disposition developed through over-dependency.

It should be remembered that a rescue dog with an unknown past may have experienced

Temperament test for rescue and re-homed dogs

This five-point test of temperament (especially developed for this book) cannot be viewed as completely reliable because a disturbed or abused dog may be displaying withdrawn behaviour. However, in most cases a dog's response to the test will give you some idea of how exposure to abuse, or the experience of the process of rescue and re-homing, may have affected a dog. Initially, maintain a distance of about a metre (3½ft) between you and the dog.

1. Hold out your hand, or hold it down by your side (so that it sems approachable to the dog) and, with soft voice, verbally encourage the dog to approach ('Good boy', 'Here', or 'Hello', or similar).

Positive: An immediate response, tail and body wagging. Hand licking.
Negative: Any suggestion of aggression or cowering. Any attempts to mouth or nip.

2. Ask to place a collar and a lead on the dog. Walk him on a close lead.
Positive: Walks by your side, without pulling or throwing himself about. Have other members of the family attempt the same.
Negative: Refuses to allow a collar and lead to placed over the head. Pulls ahead, turns away, cowers, barks or growls.

3. Instruct the dog gently, in a low tone, to sit. Stand fully erect. Do not kneel down.
Positive: Sits after the instruction has been given or by the second time of asking.
Negative: The more the instruction has to be repeated, the more negative the response.

4. Repeat the Sit instruction with the offer of a food treat. Have other members of your family undertake this part of the test.
Positive: Sits after the first instruction.
Negative: Fails to respond, suggesting that behavioural problems are acute and difficult to treat.

5. Offer the dog a toy (a ball or ring). Instruct him to give. If the dog withholds the toy, offer a food treat to encourage him to give it up.
Positive: Gives after the first instruction. Giving up after the offer of a food treat is less positive but reveals that the dog is certainly trainable.
Negative: Fails to give up the toy even when offered a food treat. suggesting that behavioural problems may be acute and difficult to treat. (Even a dog that has not been trained to recall and to give up toys is likely to drop a toy in exchange for a treat.)

Scoring

If a dog scores four out of five positives then he can be rehabilitated into a normal family environment. If a dog scores more than one negative then he should be considered difficult to rehabilitate and only a very confident dog handler should consider taking on the task.

It is also possible to test recall and obedience by throwing a ball for the dog and by calling the dog back to you once the ball has been retrieved. If the dog returns immediately and offers the ball up to you then this behaviour can be viewed as passive and obedient. If the dog returns with the ball but refuses to give it up, or drops it away from you, or doesn't even attempt to retrieve, then the dog is displaying testing or challenging behaviour. He is going to be a challenge for all but the expert to retrain. If the dog scores well on all counts, and seems generally stable, you can introduce a child (or better still two – one of each sex) to the dog. (The dog should of course remain on the lead so that there can be no direct contact.) He should have a gentle expression, with tail wagging. Any turning away or cowering, barking or growling is cause for concern.

Some aspects of this temperament test assume that the dog has undergone some level of training in the past. If a dog has not experienced any training, this should be taken into account: such a dog may fail parts of the test and still make a great adopted companion.

multiple ownership and that this can influence a dog's behaviour. There will undoubtedly have been inconsistencies in handling, which could include varied degrees of control or leadership, and lack of constancy in diet, housing, bedding, toilet rules, periods left home alone, and human and canine family (pack) size. The way in which a dog copes with his experiences can be very individual: some are more robust than others, just as some people are. Some unfortunate experiences may make one puppy more sociable and adaptable while in another they result in disturbed behaviours. Some rescue animals may have had long complicated histories and lived in the most appalling conditions, while others may have experienced only mild disruption and relatively slight problems.

The conundrums associated with an unknown past can present a challenge to even the most conscientious rescue dog owner. However, the potential for difficulties should not deter those determined to help out a canine in care. It would be an extremely disturbed dog that did not respond to consistent handling, especially when this is accompanied by the right care and attention.

If you decide to take on a rescue, always start with the assumption that the dog has suffered the worst and expect – if a canine can be described as such – a cynical animal.

The New Home

The primary care aspects of bringing your German Shepherd home remain the same whether it involves a rescue or non-rescue dog. However, the actual journey for a rescue or re-homed dog may be more emotional for both owner and puppy. Rescue dogs may already have formed a negative association with car travel, and they are more likely to be disturbed and subdued by environmental and owner changes.

The initial settling in period for a puppy in a new home is usually a week or so but it may take weeks or even months if the puppy or dog is one that is rescued or re-homed.

When you first collect a dog from a rescue organization or from his previous owner it is important to consider what the journey represents from a confused-canine viewpoint. In

A rescue or re-homed dog – whether pure-bred German Shepherd or crossbreed – doesn't have our brain capabilities and cannot possibly understand 'what or why' all the many confusing changes have occurred. It is the element of rejection by a previous human pack-member that appears to have the most lasting effect on a re-homed dog.

most cases, the dog will not know you. Nor will he understand where he is being taken or for how long. Your new friend probably cannot contemplate anything about the journey other than that it represents the 'unknown'. It is therefore potentially frightening.

The use of a covered travel or folding crate, containing an attached drink bottle with a little water, is probably the best way for the dog to travel. The least amount of fuss is best. The dog does not need cradling on someone's knee and will not appreciate the chaos that may occur through the close competing attention of young children. For this reason it is best that one adult member of the family collects the dog to keep any fuss down to a minimum.

The First Few Days
Once home the travel crate can be transferred to an appropriate space in your house (*see* Chapter 3, page 28), and the dog can be given an hour or so to take in the strange and novel smells of his new home. After a period of settling time, open the door and allow the dog to decide when to exit the travel crate. One or two members of the family could be seated close by to allow the dog to seek them out for reassurance.

Some dogs will bound out into a new home like a playful puppy, while other, more introverted characters will hesitate to leave the comfort of a confined space. It is important not to humanize the situation. Travel or folding crates that are covered and bottom-layered with a blanket represent a bolt-hole or burrow and, as such, offer the dog a secure place in a time of confusion.

The next stage is to allow the dog to explore your immediate garden, providing this area is properly fenced and there is no chance of escape. The first few days of a rescued dog's new home life will certainly be confusing, and the last thing you want is for the dog to escape into the unknown. To speed up the acceptance of his new territory the transfer of soiled newspaper, bedding material or faeces will encourage an insecure dog to mark or scent again. This can be placed into a chosen area of the garden or backyard.

On the first night, feeding the dog should not be considered a priority. Although some dogs will wolf down the first food they are offered as though they are famished, there is good reason to give low priority to offering food: on the first night the dog is likely to feel very stressed by the strangeness of the surroundings (especially if he has come from a shelter or kennels rather than from another private home) and the newness of the people.

In such circumstances a meal could trigger the onset of extremely loose bowel movements during night-time hours, and the scene that may then greet your family in the morning is likely to be very daunting. While it is vital to provide a permanent source of clean water there is no need to provide a similar bowl of food. If your dog appears willing to settle immediately it is reasonable to offer a few dry dog biscuits providing the feeding situation is controlled. Have the dog sit and offer him a biscuit or two. Even if you intend to give your new friend another type of bed, use the travel crate for the first night at least. Offer him the opportunity to relieve himself before settling down for the night.

The first meal, following diet suggestions from the rescue organization, should be offered the day after arrival, after the dog has been lead-exercised. It is very important that you follow the diet if you have been given one by the previous owner or the rescue centre. Changes in diet – especially sudden ones – can upset the digestion at the best of times. They are especially unwise when the dog is not yet settled. However, if you have no information about the dog's previous diet, it is best to choose a dry food because if the dog refuses the food initially (some do to begin with), the food can be stored in a container and offered again the following day. Do not worry if your dog does not eat immediately. He will not starve if, in the early settling-down period, he should chose to fast for a few days.

Finally, have your dog physically examined by your veterinary surgeon, who will check his overall health and condition, and give any necessary inoculations and advice.

A rescue or re-homed German Shepherd puppy or dog needs more than a few days to settle. He needs to be given plenty of time to adjust to environmental changes (perhaps a huge contrast between your home and the rescue centre or his original home). The less fuss, the fewer people or other animals to adjust to, the better the chances that he will settle into his new home and new regime and lifestyle.

Resocialization

Existing Pets
Some rescued animals are brought home to a family that already has dogs, cats and other pets. Ask those in charge of the rescue if they know whether your new friend has been socialized with other animals. If this information is not available (most likely), or if you have acquired a stray, any early contact must be organized carefully and in a controlled situation.

When another dog or puppy is introduced into an existing group there is always great potential for interaction and competition for attention, toys and food. Sometimes, with a secure dog there can simply be acceptance. Where dogs are nervous, the situation can be traumatic, with aggression, withdrawal and constant hyperactivity. This is because nervous or dominant dogs status-seek and look to test the newcomer.

You, as the owner, will know why the dogs are to be included in the family circle, but the dogs or puppies do not have human understanding of the situation and, for them, there is only confusion and nervousness. This situation is often exacerbated when the dogs being introduced are adult or when resident dogs that have made close bonds with an owner have reached sexual maturity. In human terms, it is almost like having to accept the introduction of a total stranger into the home or workplace without any formal introduction or explanation.

It is vital that early encounters with other dogs occur on neutral territory and that the new dog is not introduced to an existing dog or dogs within the confines of the home. To be neutral, the territory used for the introduction must be unfamiliar to all the dogs concerned (a new field, canal walk or woodland area). Once the dogs are in this different and exciting environment they are usually more focused on exploring, marking and scenting (territorial marking, hunting and foraging behaviours) than they are on each other. They also have to look to owners for guidance more than they do in their usual environment. To enhance the chances of this meeting on neutral ground going smoothly, it is wise to organize an 'Introduction Walk' (*see* box, page 75).

If there are no signs of aggression then the introduction to home can be achieved rapidly. Any challenge from any of the animals immediately makes integration a much slower operation.

It is possible to use travel crates to initially confine two unsocialized dogs. One can be let out and given the run of the available space within the home and garden. Then the other can take his turn. Eventually both dogs can be released together at home and shown reward, either attention or treats, for appropriate behaviour. Training discs can immediately be used to develop an association between a sound and non-reward for any unwanted aggressive behaviour. It is sometimes suggested that an existing dog or dogs should be temporarily removed from the home while the newcomer is given a chance to explore his new home without fear of confrontation over territory. However, this can still lead to competitive behaviour when the other dog is brought in. It is always advisable to make the first introduction on entirely neutral ground where social behaviour can be promoted and excess energy expelled.

Dogs that have lived in other homes or those that have experienced an extended period with a breeder can be much more difficult to establish in a new home with an existing animal. The degree of the problems likely to be encountered when re-homing is very dependent on the breed, age and per-

Josh, an adopted German Shepherd, is seen here with Jackie, his new owner, and her other dogs. However, while Josh was happy interacting with members of his own pack, he would show aggression towards other dogs outside of his group.

In this controlled-scenario session with Jackie and her friend's collie, Josh is undergoing training aimed at eliminating Josh's aggressive behaviour towards other dogs. Access to Jackie became a competitive issue during the session, but he showed improved behaviour, and this was rewarded with clicks and treats.

The Introduction Walk

1. Give all dogs involved in the socialization programme a Control Walk (each walk apart from the others). This should consist of at least a 50m/yd walk that includes about five Stops, Sits, Waits and Walk-ons (all positive responses to these instructions should be reinforced with the clicker signal and a food reward or a pat and a vocal congratulation). The ideal food treats are microwaved fatty mince or small pieces of meat and dried liver.

2. Offer a lead-walk with the dogs on parallel paths (ideally about 5m apart). Any sign of aggression should be signalled with training discs and then interrupted with the promise of a play session (show a ball, frisbee or dumb-bell) and the smell of the treats. (Click and treat all positive reactions.) It is a good idea to swap handling control of the dogs between partners (or owners if the other dog belongs to friends) to reduce any personal influence that can occur.

3. If aggression or hyperactive behaviour has not been displayed it should be possible to simultaneously release the dogs from close leads. (It may be advisable to use lunge ropes to control poor recall or any problem behaviours shown at a distance.) Walk the dogs back on the parallel route. It is vital that there is no physical or vocal contact encouraged between dogs and owners. Use a reward-whistle signal to randomly recall the dogs on a regular basis. Instruct them all to sit, offer a reward to each, and then dismiss them. Continue the walk.

4. When the walk is complete and a return is made to vehicles or to a house it is vital that the dogs are not allowed to attempt to enter together. Door thresholds and the rear of vehicles are competition triggers. Dogs are best taken separately or crated separately in the back of vehicles to prevent friction at close quarters.

5. Following the walk, socialize the dogs together in a garden or backyard. Do not inadvertently influence behaviour by standing over the dogs and expecting aggression. Any physical human presence can influence behaviour!

The more 'combined' walks that the dogs experience, the better for socialization. Ignore any excited barks or growls unless they become excessive. Interrupt problem behaviours with training discs, the promise of a treat and play, and Control Walks. Any physical aggression (biting) can be interrupted with the use of the aversion collar (*see* Chapter 6) or pepper (start sneezing and hopefully stop fighting!).

sonality of the dog. Veterinary or animal behaviour clinics will advise in each case.

Owners often adversely influence some of the behaviour by giving out the wrong signals. Nervousness or apprehension in owners is immediately signalled through body language and pheromones (skin scents) that communicate the basic emotions between animals. It is therefore important to take a positive attitude to the introduction and to have a reward signal ready and in place for good behaviour (ideally the clicker system and a reward-whistle signal that has already been randomly used).

It is always advisable to take professional advice before introducing problem dogs unless the owner is an expert dog handler or animal behaviourist.

Cats

If your rescue German Shepherd has not been socialized with cats and you have felines in the home then early introduction must be controlled and a cat given the opportunity to escape any unwanted attention. If the dog chases the cat it is vital that the dog is quickly recalled and rewarded for his return. If reliable recall has not yet been established, it is sensible to keep the dog on an extended lead during these early stages of introduction.

Puppies will usually adapt to the presence of cats and vice versa. Most of the attention

Children and secure, properly socialized GSDs go together perfectly. However, adopted dogs may have to learn the social graces expected of them, and all interactions in the first few weeks should be supervised by adults.

and quick movements that can be disturbing for any dog, let alone a nervous one that may have gone through a difficult time. Many aspects of aggression – growling, snarling, snapping, and so on, derive from fear.

The best time to introduce children to a new adult German Shepherd or crossbreed is during supervised play. The play period should be short and interesting and held in an outdoor area where the dog can be contained, such as a secure garden or hedged field. A ball game of retrieval and reward is the best method to develop a controlled relationship between dogs and young children. Lots of food reward for recall, sitting, and offering up the ball will usually cement the start of a good relationship between a nervous dog and children. It is important that any play between a child and a recently rescued dog is continually supervised and controlled by an adult.

Relationship-building

In feeling sympathetic towards a dog that has suffered the trauma of homelessness – perhaps even abuse – people often humanize the dog in that they project onto the dog the feelings they imagine they themselves would have in such circumstances. This is a mistake because while dogs do, of course, have feelings, they do not assess situations in the same way that we do. By treating the dog as a human being, you can unwittingly reinforce a distressed and confused animal's psychological problems. It is almost impossible to reassure a dog that life is not all bad by trying to stroke away problems. A dog – especially a rescued dog – should be treated as a dog: with firmness and consistency as well as kindness.

The first few weeks in a new home are the most important, especially when it comes to establishing a secure territory and a healthy owner–pet relationship. Dogs do not wander around stroking and patting each other.

on both sides will be based on natural curiosity and play. Some adult dogs will have been encouraged to chase cats, and it may take some close and repetitive training to change or counter-condition this behaviour. Sometimes a dog may be very friendly with your own cat, and yet chase others away from your garden, but this has more to do with territory protection than aggression. Cats can usually get the better of dogs, and long-term problems are unlikely in all but a few cases.

Young Children and Strange Dogs

Introducing a rescue dog to young children should also be carefully planned. Some rescue dogs are nervous of small humans for a number of good reasons. In their past they may have been tormented by children. Or it may simply be that they have never been exposed to young children in their previous home. Young children can be extremely unpredictable: they make loud, sudden noises

This GSD-cross, Rocky, had to undergo extensive behavioural treatment (see page 114). Here he is seen rolling over and exposing his vulnerable underbelly to comunicate his submissiveness to his owner.

Whatever we may like to think, this aspect of our relationship with dogs is mainly for the benefit of humans and not for the animals. Stroking a dog can be a stress-buster for humans: it can lower our blood pressure and reduce heart rate. For a secure dog in a stable relationship with his owner, a good supply of pats and strokes is accepted as an expression of human approval and as part of human behaviour. It's what the master wants! To an insecure and disorientated dog, excessive stroking and patting can be seen as confusing and will exacerbate attention seeking, insecurity and anxiety.

It is better to be detached and unemotional about a rescue or re-homed dog in the first few months until a family is absolutely sure that the dog has settled into the home and lifestyle. The dog must be trustworthy not only with his owner but also with any children, strangers, other dogs, and all family members and friends.

It is admirable that people should want to make up for the difficult life that a rescued dog may have suffered. However, such kindness should be channelled into providing company, good food, warm bedding, and plenty of controlled walks. Now that's a list that all dogs can appreciate and understand. All dogs offered food and a home coupled with firm and consistent control will respond to their owners in a positive way. Your consistency is all-important because this will shine through and become apparent to the dog long before any other attribute you may have to share with your new canine chum.

Establishing the 'Pack'

A rescue dog will arrive in your home with three simple canine questions, and these will need answering sooner rather than later. These questions are usually:

- 'What's my place in this new human-canine pack?'
- 'Who is in charge?' (male or female); and
- 'What do I have to do in order to get what I want?'

Use height to express dominance over a dog. In difficult situations where hyperactivity may be a problem, offer a toy to attract his attention.

A dreadful combination of nervous or aggressive behaviours can develop when a dog doesn't get the answers to these questions. This is especially true if the dog has been successful in the past by being extrovert or aggressive (*see* Chapter 6).

Sometimes antisocial behaviour in a rescue dog is put down to a dominance problem. It is true that challenging and aggressive behaviours may be exhibited when a dog is dominant and has experienced poor socialization. However, the same can be said of a dog that is not naturally dominant but doesn't know his place within the human-canine pack. This

type of dog is much better referred to as one that is 'status-seeking'. Provided such a dog knows and acknowledges who is in charge then antisocial behaviours will reduce and, ultimately, be extinguished.

Sometimes a rescue dog will immediately attempt to form a strong attachment with an owner, and then the strong bonding leads to uncertainty about his place within the perceived pack (the family). A dominant dog may consider himself to be – or hope to find himself – in an alpha (leader's) role within the family. This dog would then believe that certain areas or items in the home – such as a bed, toys, the garden, and so on – are his territory and possessions. Such a dog may also perceive some family members as subordinate, and this is a recipe for disaster. Without firm handling and absolute control, this type of dog will prove to be entirely unsuitable for an average family seeking a loyal companion.

In many cases it is frustration that can create many behavioural problems in dogs. The particular frustration may be linked to the relationship (not knowing his place in the human-canine pack), or to access to food, or even to a general lack of mental stimulation.

A challenging dog may believe his role is to control and protect the human-canine pack. Aggressive behaviour can also be food-associated or triggered by a target that is seen as 'threatening'. It is vital that a re-homed German Shepherd is shown that he does not need to protect property or control any of the people within the home or on walks. If an owner allows territorial behaviour it will be displayed when it is least wanted or expected.

There is no point giving a powerful, nervous dog what I can only describe as 'wishy-washy' boundaries (soft voice and gentle tugs on the lead) that may vary from day to day depending on how you are feeling. It is essential for the dog to be secure in a home environment and for him to clearly understand that his place is at the bottom of the pack. A testing dog can sense hesitation, apprehension, anxiety or fear shown by any family members or friends, so confident and consistent handling is necessary.

Communicating Leadership

A rescue German Shepherd Dog will be desperate for leadership and firm but fair, consistent handling. It is very much like dealing with a disruptive child (although the dog is not as complex). The dog needs clear boundaries to indicate what is correct and what is wrong behaviour.

Showing a dog who is boss is not about rough handling, shouting or being a bully. It is about being firm, fair, consistent and calm. Your tone of voice should be bright when the dog responds positively to instructions. A low-toned voice is necessary when correcting problem behaviour and in order to show dominance. For example, handling problems during lead-walking should be addressed by issuing low-toned instructions alongside a sharp tug on the lead. Always use a head-control collar on an adopted dog. This way, you will be able to control pulling behaviour from the very first walk. This will in itself confirm your leadership.

It is important to ignore the dog outside of feeding, play and walk interactions. The 'power of ignore' outside these times is highly effective in promoting good behaviour. It is vital that family members and friends generally ignore your dog for the first month whilst controlled socializing is being undertaken. During this period, minimize any potential triggers for hyperactivity, excitability or aggression and restrict contact to:

• Expressing control and 'dominance'.
• Giving calming signals, which will encourage a dog to rest and be less anxious.

Ignoring a dog should not be confused with the 'silent treatment' that is meted out by humans to a family member or friend as a means of expressing hurt, anger, or general unhappiness about the relationship. To canines, a dog that ignores other dogs is expressing dominance ('I'm a top dog or wolf and I don't bother with the likes of lower members of the pack'), or indicating that there is nothing pack-wise going on – no mating, no hunting and foraging, no challenges for pack position, and so on. The canine 'ignore' behaviour is all about conserving energy and being calm. That is why this strategy is vital to calming a nervous dog. Your detached calmness towards a German Shepherd Dog will not say: 'I don't love you any more' or 'You have done something wrong' (unless of course you are also sending out signals of disappointment or anger).

The importance of not allowing a German Shepherd to occupy raised platforms or other positions that offer a guarding advantage or physical elevation is especially relevant when dealing with rescue dogs. Reduce any possibility for the dog to guard from any vantage position by not allowing him to sit on furniture or to sleep on the stairs or near bedrooms and beds. It is recommended that a stair-gate is used to prevent stairs and upper room access.

Elevation, and close proximity to owners at sleeping times, can cause a disorientated dog to become confused; to a naturally dominant dog it offers a psychological advantage. Make sure that the dog does not jump up at you, or your visitors and others, by using the clicker and training discs (*see* Chapter 4). In addition, do not lower yourself, or allow others, to descend to the dog's height, and avoid floor-play and same-height confrontations. It is also advisable to impose time-out periods (in an indoor covered crate) to discourage the dog from seeking excessive attention.

Be Prepared

In adopting a dog you are likely to observe problems in behaviour. It is unwise to consider taking on a dog, especially one whose history is not fully known, without being prepared for this.

An owner of a rescue dog needs to use a simple communication system that will immediately inform the dog what is expected and what is not expected in terms of behaviour. Adopted dogs invariably need reward incentives and clear signals from new owners. Be ready to reward any good behaviour with the clicker signal system. This signal should be accompanied with a fuss or a food treat, pats alongside vocal congratulations, and 'Yes' in a bright voice. Be prepared to signal any problem behaviours with the use of training discs and a firm, low-toned 'No'. The dog will soon learn. German Shepherd Dogs are usually very quick to learn when complex instructions, ambiguity and inconsistency are eliminated.

The rescue dog might be compared to the troubled child that expresses his frustration with bad behaviour. Think of a rescue German Shepherd in the same way but do not assume that you can 'talk' the troubles better. The dog doesn't have a voice and so he cannot express directly, in human language, any confusion, distrust or distress that has been experienced during the rescue and re-homing phase. The dog may attention-seek and may show naughty behaviour to induce a reaction from family members and friends, such as running off with items in the hope that you will give chase. In my clinical research, the items are often human-scented, with the top ten targets being trainers, shoes, slippers, underwear, socks, towels, hankies, tissues, mobile phones, and remote controls. By handling or wearing these items we effectively 'mark' them with

our body scent, which is why dogs are attracted to them.

Sometimes the dog's hyperactive behaviour may trigger a drama. On other occasions the dog may frustrate or even anger an owner. These human reactions make the game more exciting for the dog. A highly instinctive German Shepherd may attempt to exploit any chaos (such as unexpected visitors arriving) and any weakness shown by you, your family and friends (there is always someone who loves dogs and who cannot be told that the dog hasn't to be fussed in order to prevent hyperactivity). This exploitation of the moment is not 'nastiness'; it is simply an attempt to make full use of any social opportunities that come along. The dog doesn't know how, why or when 'exciting moments' will come, but he is usually quick enough to recognize and make the most of them when they do.

For many such situations it is advisable to use a distraction strategy so that you psychologically interrupt the dog and turn the situation into one that can be controlled. The best methods to use for interrupting mild problem behaviours, such as stealing personal items, are the reward whistle and training discs, as described in Chapter 4. It is also possible to bring out the dog lead and then briefly walk the dog around the house or rustle a food bag and offer a treat when the dog's curiosity will make him turn his attention back to you. If these actions are used casually and not directly at the dog then interruption will be successful because a dog wants to interact with an owner.

Like the dysfunctional child, a rescue or re-homed German Shepherd Dog will respond positively to consistency, fair handling and a reward system for good behaviour. Simply be prepared for problem behaviour and deal with it calmly and positively. With these rules it is possible to eventually guide a dog into becoming an ideal companion.

6   Problem Behaviour

When the world has treated a German Shepherd Dog badly it is no surprise that behavioural problems follow. Perhaps a neglected dog has already been exposed to problems at the litter stage (poor socialization, premature removal from the litter, poor environment, and so on). In many cases in my clinic the dog is driven by basic frustrations and confusions, and it has been recognized that changes in homes and people around a dog, or onset of illness in the owner, may trigger behavioural problems. Sometimes a dog has been exposed to inconsistent handling as a puppy and an immature or poor litter mother. In the worst cases, the dog has been exposed to abuse and cruelty, confusion, aggression, environmental extremes, extreme weather conditions, danger and starvation. Under any of these conditions a dog (and humans for that matter) will almost always revert to instinct in order to adapt and survive.

The exposure to problem situations and events will affect a dog in one of two distinct ways: the dog either becomes withdrawn (depressed in a canine diagnosis), or he will develop nervous and fear-based aggressive tendencies.

It is important to understand that any continued aggressive behaviour displayed by a dog suggests that he is not happy and content in the world. Unless you intend to keep a German Shepherd specifically as a guard dog – and wish to encourage aggression as a threat to trespassers – it is important to realize that such behaviours are antisocial and unwanted. This book assumes that you want to own a companion animal (rather than a guard dog) that will not be a threat to anyone or any other animal.

Classification of Aggression in Canines

Aggressions can be directed towards other dogs, to owners and family members, or to strangers. It is possible to classify the various types of canine aggression into four main groups:

1. Intraspecific (dog versus dog).

2. Predatory (attack and bite).

3. Possessive (growling over food or toys and refusing to give up items).

4. Protective (responding to perceived threat to the owner or family members), fear-based, target and territorial (towards strangers, moving targets, and property and grounds).

A nervous or challenging dog is often in a permanent state of hyper-alertness (ready for any threat – real or not) and he will usually

About aggression

Aggression in all animals is rewarded in two distinct ways:

1. It offers an advantage in reproduction or in gaining food or territory.

2. Something feared is 'driven away' or 'escaped' from, following which the animal is rewarded by 'chemical' relief – serotonin – in the brain.

1. Dominant or challenging aggression
This type of aggression is about a dog wanting to be the boss, wanting to compete, and needing to be first all the time. This dog will always be status-seeking or challenging for a higher place in the human-canine pack.

Status-seeking behaviour can be seen in elements of play (when the dog dictates terms, such as not giving up a ball or returning it), in attempting to control access to food and toys (growling and being possessive over a bone, chew or toy), and in occupying vantage points (on top of the stairs, on the settee or chair, and so on). Another clear sign of challenging or potentially dominant behaviour is when the dog demands to go through doorways and thresholds before an owner.

2. Fear-based aggression
Fear-based aggression derives from adrenaline-driven responses that support the 'flight, freeze or fight' modes of behaviour. This hormonal

system has evolved to aid survival in nature. Adrenaline is an extremely powerful chemical that rapidly stimulates the brain in order to speed up survival responses. Many rescue and re-homed dogs would appear to have permanently high levels of adrenaline, which can quickly be triggered to flood the nervous dog's brain. It is as though the dog is in a state of permanently fighting for survival: a condition that I refer to as 'hyper-alertness'. Such dogs are always 'on the edge', waiting for the worst to happen. When a nervous German Shepherd has excess levels of adrenaline in his brain system, he is a loaded gun.

Once a 'potential problem' has been dealt with (barked at, chased off or escaped from) then other chemical mechanisms in the brain help a dog to feel calmer. The intensity of relief gained by some dogs by the success in chasing off a perceived threat (another dog, postman, someone on a bike) can be greater than any possible practical 'benefit' that may have been gained from his aggressive action. This is why the behaviour can quickly develop into addiction, especially if there is an increase in the frequency of the bouts of aggression. The dog believes he has 'seen off' the threat and that perception makes the dog feel the aggressive response has been successful. *We* know that the postman or paperboy has gone next door to deliver more letters or newspapers, but the dog cannot understand this and cannot disassociate the apparent departure from his behaviour.

growl at, bark, lunge, snap, nip at, or chase off any target that he considers threatening to the human-canine pack or territory (passers-by, delivery personnel and so on). People and dogs often leave the scene following the bout of aggressive behaviour, and this only reinforces the dog's idea that he has succeeded in 'chasing off' a perceived threat. Aggression towards other dogs can develop when a dog has been challenged by or attacked by another dog either at the early puppy stages or as an adult. Fear of attack often promotes a 'get in first' type of behav-

iour that can be linked to fear aggression. Such aggression can also be promoted by hyperactive, adrenalin-driven behaviour.

Whilst all these canine behaviours are instinctive and potentially addictive (because a dog is relieved to have dealt with or escaped from a threat following a bout of aggression), the behaviour may have been learned in the dog's early stages of development. If the litter mother or other family dogs display aggressive behaviours then the puppies quickly imitate them. Aggression in dogs can also be inadvertently encouraged by nerv-

A young dog will normally express submissive behaviour to an older adult dog. Here, Bess is mouth-licking to display her understanding of her lower position with the adult dogs in her group.

ous, inconsistent or passive control on the part of the owner, and by insecurity.

Status-seeking or Dominant Behaviours

The word 'dominance' is certainly overused in discussions on canine antisocial behaviour, especially with reference to strong-willed or aggressive German Shepherd Dogs. The so-called dominant dog may well have been the 'pick of the litter', potentially an alpha male in nature. However, it doesn't matter how important the dog may believe himself to be. It is relevant only that the 'testing dog' should know he is never as important as his owners. In the main, the subject of dominant dogs has been dealt with in Chapter 5 in the section about the dog learning to know his place within the human-canine pack.

A number of dogs are not dominant but simply status-seeking in that they are unsure of the status of some or all of the family members in relation to themselves. I have always likened the status-seeking domesticated dog to the naughty child who is testing his parents. Although dogs do not have anything like the brainpower of a child they are sometimes asking the same questions: 'How much can I get away with?' and, 'If I behave in this way will I get what I want?'

Dogs are genetically programmed to seek out and find their place within the pack environment, and in the absence of the 'true pack' a family becomes the ideal replacement. Testing or challenging dogs are not being simply nasty. Often they are confused about their role in the human-canine pack and need only to be instructed, in canine language, which members are in charge. In

If there are any concerns about a dog's temperament and aggressive behaviour then it is advisable to use a muzzle.

(linked to fear, which triggers adrenalin) should have been decreased by reduced owner attention and by limiting the opportunities for the dog to display aggression.

Target Aggression

When dealing with a dog that displays a particular gender or age bias linked to nervous aggression you will need someone who can represent the particular target person that triggers aggression.

The followng scenarios are intended to teach the dog that not all strangers or targets for fear-based aggression are a threat. Start the retraining in a neutral area such as a field or neighbour's garden. Once a dog begins to show calmness in the vicinity of a potential target, the process can be repeated in the

home or garden. During the sessions it is essential that everyone remains calm, relaxed and in possession of a clicker and dog treats.

Control Scenario 1: Outside the Home

1. Ask the potential target person and child to approach from the side. As they do so, instruct the dog firmly to sit. Reward obedience with a treat or a pat. Click and treat (repeatedly) all appropriate behaviour.

   If the dog fixes a stare, or growls or barks at the person, first sound training discs, then attract the dog's attention with a novel toy or the reward whistle.

2. Once the dog's attention has been gained (this can be with the use of a favourite toy) the firm instruction 'Sit!' should be used again and the dog should be rewarded for obedience. At any sign of nervous aggression, such as hackles raised, growling, barking or lungeing, it is important to sound the training discs, show a food reward but remove it, and then momentarily suspend the retraining session.

3. Providing the dog is under control (with little or no excitability shown towards the target person), allow the person to approach. If you are confident with the situation, the target person can click and treat the dog in the Sit position, then step away and instruct the dog to approach him while you walk forward with the dog on the lead. The target person must then instruct the dog to sit, and then click and reward the dog with a food treat or a toy (throw a frisbee or ball or dumb-bell, which should be replaced on retrieval with a food treat). Following this event the target person should ignore the dog and walk away. Repeat the training with various people in different environments.

Control Scenario 2:
Inside the Home

When Control Scenario 1 has succeeded, arrange for a potential target and child to visit the home. The time must be established beforehand (a quiet evening or early morning period, when there are as few other distractions as possible).

1. Just before the prearranged time, sit and recall the dog several times in a click-and-treat session. When the actors arrive, they should knock on the door or ring the doorbell once. When, or if, the dog rushes to the door, first sound the training discs and say a firm 'No'. Next, sound the reward whistle (the signal to recall and reward) to interrupt his behaviour.

   The visitors must wait until the dog's behaviour has been successfully interrupted and the owner is ready for the next stage (with the dog recalled and sat).

2. Slowly walk to the door with the dog and praise any calmness. Instruct the dog to sit, and click and treat a good response. Slowly open the door with the dog instructed to sit and stay. The visitors should be calmly encouraged to enter with a basic greeting but they should ignore the dog.

3. Once in the room of choice, instruct the dog to sit. Click, and offer a reward of a food treat. Ask the visitors not to give eye contact to the dog but, if he has responded obediently, they should also offer a repeated click and food session.

   Following success with this event everyone must then ignore the dog.

4. Place the dog in his indoor kennel or crate (or in his bed). The dog should remain there until a few minutes before the visitors are about to leave. Instruct the

dog to sit before the guests for a final click-and-treat session. Always praise the dog in a bright voice and offer a stroke, click and food treat for all good responses.

Some dogs also display territorial and/or fear aggression towards visitors when they are leaving. This is because nervous dogs are 'rewarded' by relief (linked to a chemical reward in the brain) after they have 'chased off' the 'intruders'.

In these cases, have the dog's favourite toy or food treat ready (in my clinic cases this has been a favourite teddy bear, ball, ring, carrot, chew, or bone) to use as a distraction tool. A member of the family should hold on to this item to gain the dog's attention while another member leads the guests away. If you are retraining a dog alone, as the solitary owner, approach the door calmly with the item visible to the dog and instruct him to sit at the door and allow the visitors to exit. Praise any calm behaviour and reward the dog with the item and a firm pat and a food treat. Praise in a bright voice and stroke or click and treat all correct responses. Problem behaviour should be signalled with the training discs and the session ended on a positive note.

This process should be repeated as many times as possible so that the association between visitors, strangers and children and the dog become positive and more rewarding. Training discs can be used at any stage to signal and interrupt problem behaviours.

In the early days of the retraining, it is recommended that you remove the dog *before* strangers arrive and leave to prevent the dog from experiencing a successful confrontation and to reduce the frustration at being excluded from social family meetings.

Control Scenario 3:
Attacking Post

If the dog has an addiction to attacking letters or newspapers as they are being delivered, set up a scenario in which a person delivers a letter or paper while the owner works on interruption, recall and reward using training discs, clicker and whistle.

The dog must be prevented from being rewarded by his behaviour, which is a mix of fear-based and territorial aggression. A dog gate in the hallway will help prevent a dog from obtaining his 'fix', and the addiction to this behaviour can be significantly reduced,

Any sign of aggression (indoor or outdoor) shown by the dog should be immediately signalled with a firm 'No' and followed by the sound of training discs. Show the dog a food or toy reward and then remove the item until suitable behaviour is displayed.

Intraspecific Aggression

German Shepherd Dogs that are displaying a range of nervous behaviours discussed in this chapter have usually experienced difficulties during their early socialization period (sometimes because of rescue or re-homing). When these behaviours are shown towards other dogs, they are known as intraspecific aggression. This type of canine aggression, when displayed by dogs that have been dominated or bullied by another dog within the home environment, can be difficult to change. The bullied dog will often display aggression towards other dogs when they are encountered outdoors.

The behaviour of the other dog encountered on walks and in these situations will often dictate how a nervous dog reacts. If the other dog approaches, 'stands', licks his mouth and wags his tail (both calming signals) without attempting to pick up an anal scent, then this behaviour may be interpreted as non-challenging and as an invitation to join a chase (forage). Sometimes the stance will be interpreted as dominance (especially if it is 'stiff' and there is eye-to-eye contact) and it may then be considered challenging.

If an approaching dog immediately attempts to sniff the dog and then growls or barks, this will often trigger a nervous dog into an aggressive challenge or full fight.

It is extremely difficult to change the way a dog responds towards strange dogs encountered on walks if they show aggressive behaviour. However, it is often possible to change or counter-condition aggressive behaviour on the part of your dog if the strange dog does not show aggression.

To begin with, work should be done to make the dog feel more secure in his own environment. It is then possible to begin to desensitize the dog to the presence of other dogs and therefore discourage him from attacking, lungeing or barking at them. If a dog is hyperactive or over-excited before a walk then adrenalin levels in the brain will affect the degree of aggressiveness, so it is essential to promote calmness before you set out.

Control Scenario:
Dog meets Dog:

Some nervous or dominant dogs are more inclined to display excitability and aggression towards other dogs when on the lead. This may be because a dog is frustrated at being held back from an encounter or because he interprets the restricted movement of the other dog as 'stand-offishness' or dominance. The following therapy should be initially undertaken with all dogs restrained on short, simple, strap-type leads.

Ask a friend or neighbour who has a non-aggressive dog to help. It is important that this other dog is calm, pleasant-natured and perfectly happy in his family, and that the territory on which the dogs are to meet is neutral. By using a calm dog for the procedure it will be possible to teach your dog that not all other dogs are 'threatening'. If your dog is powerful and has previously displayed extreme bouts of aggression towards other dogs it is advisable to use a muzzle to

When establishing a scenario to counter aggression towards other dogs, it is important that the sociable – or 'control' – dog used is not dominant and will therefore not react adversely when any problem behaviours are shown.

ensure everyone's peace of mind. It is important that the event is properly controlled: the greater the number of factors controlled, the better the chance of changing the dog's antisocial response.

1. Firstly, give your dog a Control Walk (*see* Chapter 4) away from the neutral place chosen for the controlled encounter. Then take your dog to the meeting place.

2. Encourage the dog to sit, and repeatedly reward obedience with reassurance and a food treat.

3. When the other dog comes into view, slacken the hold on the lead and remain relaxed. Any apprehension felt by an owner is directly transmitted to the dog through the lead and by scent signals. When the dog is clearly under control (sitting) offer a further reward (treat or toy) as the other dog is walked (side on) and past at a distance of about 10m (11yd).

Maintain the antisocial dog in a sideways-on position to the other dog. This will prevent the other dog from appearing dominant or challenging to yours. If the other dog is of calm easy-going temperament, this positioning should not provoke him into being aggressive.

Clicks and treats can be continually offered to the dog as reward for appropriate behaviour and to aid distraction. *Praise* all appropriate behaviour. It is important that any excited behaviour is ignored as any attention given can inadvertently reinforce and reward it.

a visible level of arousal (excitement, barking, panting and so on).

2. Halt the dog's progress and give clear, control instructions such as Stop, Heel and Sit. Once the desired response and attention has been achieved you can offer the dog several click and reward signals such as a pat, food treat or vocal congratulation. Initially, the reward should be significant (fresh meat, liver treat or the offer of play with a new toy).

3. If the dog immediately pulls towards the target when it first comes into view, attract the dog's attention with the reward whistle or a novel toy. Once his attention has been regained, instruct the dog to sit, and reward him for obedience. Any acute signs of excitability, nervousness or aggression should be signalled with the training discs or aversion collar and the session immediately suspended until another day.

4. Take a Control Walk immediately afterwards so that the session ends on a positive, rewarded, note.

Over a series of short sessions, the distance between the dog and the 'triggers' can be reduced until, eventually, the dog does not show excessive arousal and obeys control commands. Do not progress to the next level without achieving the previous level. All positive responses (attention focused on the owner rather than on the target) should be clicked and rewarded.

In acute cases, aversion punishment can be used if the dog does not respond to retraining. You may wish to take professional advice at this stage.

Refusal to Recall

If a dog refuses to respond to recall, you will need to supervise him with the use of a lunge-line, or extending lead, and a head-control collar. Dogs that display target aggression will also need a muzzle during walks where dogs or strangers are encountered and aggression is likely to be displayed. This level of supervision can be reduced after a period of months when the dog has clearly learned new routines and has dramatically improved recall response during walks.

Positive behaviour and good responses should be repeatedly clicked and treated. It is important not to make any event of disobedience, hyperactivity, or aggression exciting by offering a dog excessive attention as this will only turn the event into a game and will encourage problem behaviours.

Always attempt to finish a session on a positive note with a well-rewarded click and treat Control Walk or a very brief retrieval session with a ball (two or three throws).

Hyper-attachment and Over-dependency

The term Separation-related Disorder (SRD) or anxiety is a term to describe the behaviour of a dog that cannot bear the emotional disturbance that separation from his 'pack' creates, so he cannot be left in the home without problem behaviours being displayed. The condition is common amongst rescue and re-homed dogs, especially where there has been attachment to a previous owner, but it can easily develop in dogs that have made a strong bond with a new individual.

Usually, the first indication that separation problems are developing is when the owner leaves the dog for an extended period and, upon return, discovers evidence of the dog's disturbed behaviour. In the case of a puppy some behaviours are difficult to distinguish from normal behaviour, such as boredom, toilet-training mishaps, and fretting behaviour.

There are three very distinct behavioural signs of SRD (*see* box right). One or more of the three behaviours occur when the dog is left alone, sometimes even when people are in the home but are asleep or in a different room. Research into the syndrome suggests that for SRD-linked behaviours to be displayed it is not critical whether a dog is left for five minutes or five hours. In rare cases, the same behaviours can also be shown when family members are around and this can sometimes disguise or conceal the true nervous condition.

Coming to Terms with Separation

Firstly, in order to help reduce a German Shepherd Dog's dependency and to deal with any distress he may be displaying in an owner's absence, it is important to encourage the dog to be alone in a room, ideally in a covered dog crate to restrict the dog's movements, or in his dog bed or backyard/garden while the owners remain in the house.

Without the use of the 'den effect', such as a covered folding crate or indoor kennel, treatment is much more difficult. Dogs suffering from SRD usually respond adversely to enforced sessions of controlled separation by displaying inappropriate urination and defecation, excessive vocalization and destructive behaviours. If the dog has freedom of space to perform these various behaviours then they quickly become habitual, self-rewarding and, ultimately, addictive.

If it is possible to leave the dog alone for short periods of time to offer a gradual change then do so. Following the isolation session, instruct the dog to sit, and click and praise any progress after ten minutes following your return. Use the clicker to signal reward, and give a special food treat, if the dog has not barked or shown signs of destructiveness (or inappropriate urination). Gradually increase the period of time a dog suffering from the condition is left alone.

The three clinical signs of SRD

1. Excessive vocalization, such as howling, whining and/or barking

Any howling is a dog calling 'wolf-style' to the owner. Barking is alert calling, whereas whining is submissive plea behaviour. Eventually, whatever the vocalization that has been used by a dog, the owner will return: the dog then considers that his behaviour has been successful, so he will repeat it upon every separation.

2. Inappropriate urination and defecation

Any inappropriate urination and defecation is rarely a need to toilet for dogs but more an urge to 'mark the territory' during a nervous bout brought on by separation. A dog receives chemical relief in his brain when marking the territory. This behaviour can sometimes be confused with 'faulty learning' (*see* Chapter 3).

3. Scratching, excessive digging and chewing

This manifests itself in two distinct forms: attempting to access where the owner has last been seen (doors and door frames); and discharging the 'emotion' of separation by chewing inappropriate items such as furniture, wires, human-scented soft furnishings, and bedding and so on. In some cases the dog digs and scratches into carpets and floorboards.

The destructive scratching or chewing is often frustration driven, but it can be a panic response to what appears to the dog to be abandonment. It is not vandalism as we know it in human terms. Destructive and excessive chewing behaviour can become obsessive and compulsive in some dogs because the repetitiveness of the action becomes addictive. When a behaviour (such as scratching or chewing the door or door frame or carpet) is repeated, it is known that the brain triggers the release of a 'reward' chemical, which stimulates the dog to repeat the behaviour over and over again, in effect giving rise to a vicious cycle. Research has shown that chewing behaviours probably also have a calming effect on dogs in much the same way that chewing gum aids human concentration.

Andrew and Dougal are the best of friends in the companion animal sense. Typically for an adopted dog, he has formed a powerful attachment (hyper-attachment or hyperbonding) to his owner, which makes even the shortest separation period emotional for him.

Create a timetable

It is important to establish a fixed timetable for separation periods to be enforced while you are at home with the dog. The periods can begin as 20-minute sessions and then build up into hourly ones. The increments used would depend on how acute the condition is suffered by a dog.

These sessions should be developed over a period of six to eight weeks. The process cannot be rushed. When periods of enforced separation are acceptable to the dog for seven to fourteen days they can be increased for the next week or fortnight.

Keep any greetings contact down to a minimum. Most pet owners are flattered by excessive greetings from dogs because it is interpreted as faithfulness and great pleasure at the reunion, confirming that the pet has missed his owner. However, such hyperactivity can turn mild SRD into an acute condition.

It is vital in cases of SRD that the dog is not fussed or given too much attention first thing in the morning or on exit or entrance to the home. This strategy helps to reduce the contrast between an owner's presence and absence. Any hyperactivity stimulated prior to an owner leaving, or after his return, will create a surge of adrenalin-generated excitement for a nervous dog. Such bursts of activity can only highlight the difference between an owner's presence and absence and will add to any emotional disturbance the

Rocky enjoyed his temporary 'den' so much that he made his own modifications to enhance the 'safe and snug' effect.

dog experiences when the owner is away. A pat and a click and food-treat should be given in reward for sitting at least 15 minutes before your departure and again after a dog has settled down following your return.

Combating SRD Triggers
The aim is to make the separation from an owner as comfortable as possible for the dog. To help in this, you can do the following:

- Reduce any signals or cues that 'announce' departure. Have hats, coats, keys and shoes ready in advance.
- Consider more obscure cues: setting house alarms and answer machines, closing doors and starting vehicles.
- Make a toy, chew or uncooked bone available to reduce any potential boredom. An interactive self-rewarding

toy such as a foraging ball can offer a distraction during periods of isolation. These should always be removed a shortly after your return home in order to maintain their novelty value.
- Avoid offering such chews, treats or interactive toys immediately prior to leaving. Instead, about half an hour before departure, leave any of these potential boredom-reducing items available for the dog to discover later while you are away.
- Sometimes offer treats or other items (that have become associated with your leaving the house) at random times when you are not leaving home. Sometimes put a coat on and handle keys as if to go out, but then remain in the home.
- Background 'talk' helps to reduce hyper-alertness in nervous dogs. To make the

Dougal, adopted by Andrew from a family member, has suffered from Separation-related Disorder for several years. The marks on the door confirm one of the known signs of the condition, where a dog becomes distressed when an owner leaves the home.

separation period and/or absence less defined, leave a television or talk-radio programme playing in the background before, during and after your departure and return to home. This strategy will prevent the turning on and off of the radio from becoming a cue to separation.

When the introduction of separation periods has proved successful, you can attempt to leave the dog alone in the house. However, you should return almost immediately, ignore the dog for a short period, then praise and reward calm behaviour. The period of separation can then be gradually increased over time. After an extended absence, aim to avoid interaction with the dog for 15 to 20 minutes before leaving, and upon returning home, as this will help to reduce the contrast between your presence and absence.

In acute cases, dogs may require the support of drug therapy (*see* box opposite). This can be discussed with a vet if it is considered necessary. Ideally, a dog suffering from SRD should not be left for any extended period that has not yet been experienced and learned through controlled separation.

Shadowing behaviour
A dog that always needs to be physically close – 'shadowing' his owner – creates a great deal of potential for interaction between owner and dog. There is often a hidden agenda behind a dog's need to be so close. While all dogs need to be a part of the perceived human-canine pack, a nervous, clingy dog seeks excessive closeness in the attempt to increase his own status.

Competition for attention will be intensified at times when visitors first arrive in the

Drug therapy for Separation-related Disorder

Drug therapies are available for acute cases of excessive nervousness and SRD. However, the use of these treatments should be considered carefully. I have successfully treated hundreds of dogs with the condition without the use of drug therapy, and I believe that drugs should be used only if behavioural therapy alone fails to treat the condition. I do not take drugs needlessly, and I do not believe that animals should be any different in this respect.

If, having said this, a decision is made to use a drug therapy, and it is to be successfully employed, it is important that the dog has controlled play and walk sessions to stimulate the production of seratonin – the naturally forming reward chemical in the brain. The drugs work by suppressing the reabsorption of seratonin so that this 'reward chemical' is retained in the brain for longer than is normal. This is why these antidepressants are described in human terms as 'happy drugs'.

home, and when the family are excited about events and are leaving or arriving frequently. Close contact during these times will be seen as reward by a dog. For this reason it is important to discourage excessive closeness, excitement (jumping up, barking and so on) or patrolling or guarding. House thresholds – such as doorways, gates and stairs – will often be challenged or guarded, depending on how much the dog is 'testing' his status.

Coprophagia

Coprophagia – the eating of faeces (either an animal's own or another animal's) – has its roots in instinctive behaviour for recycling and foraging for food in nature. There is little reference to the phenomenon in commercial literature, so many dogs have been taken to veterinary surgeons for euthanasia by horrified owners as a result of

this behaviour being observed in domesticated, companion dogs.

There is some debate about the real cause of coprophagia in domesticated canines, and there are a number of suspected causes (*see* box, page 98). It is believed by some behaviour experts to be linked to a diet lacking in certain vitamins or minerals, and some have advised that it is helpful to feed a diet high in fibre and protein and low in carbohydrate. However, I believe the diet theory could be a red herring and, if your dog is currently on a balanced and varied diet, nutritional cause is in any case unlikely.

Combating Coprophagia

Aim to restrict or control where and when your puppy or dog can defecate so that you can have some control of the situation. Always bear in mind that there is the potential for inadvertent reinforcement by humans: for the dog, an angry or disgusted reaction can represent attention and can encourage repetition of the behaviour.

Crating, and behavioural treatment supervised by a qualified animal behaviourist, will in the long term usually eliminate the behaviour occurring in an owner's absence. There are also some practical guidelines that you can follow to assist you in combating the problem:

1. If you are present when defecation occurs within the home or garden territory, remove or crate the dog away from the event in another room while the faeces are removed and cleaning is undertaken. If you clean up out of the dog's sight, it will help to prevent the inadvertent 'owner competition', which is known to be a potential reinforcement of the condition.

2. Use a biological spray cleaner rather than a strong disinfectant as the former tends to reduce the dog's desire to re-mark the original soiling site.

Suggested causes of coprophagia in dogs

Coprophagia may be caused by a combination of factors, which may include some of the following:

- Faulty learning during the litter stage (first six weeks) or during the post-litter stage when the puppy has observed the litter mother, or other dogs kept in the same environment, eating their faeces.
- The availability and or access to the faeces of other animals (cats, dogs, horses and pets) during the litter and post-litter stage.
- The experience of a poor environment during the early stages of a puppy's development, such as inappropriate confinement in a small pen, backyard or outbuilding, overcrowding, excessive competition for food, large litters, mixed litters, pet shops, puppy farms, rescue centres, and so on.
- Starvation; inadequate, poor or inappropriate diet during the litter and post-litter stages.
- Boredom as a result of under-stimulation.
- Separation-related Disorder, where the puppy or dog has made a powerful attachment onto an owner and family members and is distressed during their absence.
- There may be a link to overactive anal gland problems (*see* Chapter 7) and hormone scents.

3. Do not help to make the event 'exciting' or dramatic by making a lot of fuss or becoming angry.

4. If you observe the dog defecating, interrupt the faeces-eating behaviour *before* coprohagic behaviour can commence by sounding training discs. Then sound a reward whistle, or squeaky toy. This signal should have already been established over several days as being linked to a food reward but not to the problem behaviour. Call him to you and give the Sit in-

struction. Click and offer a special food treat for this obedience.

Always distract the dog after defecation with reward-whistle recall, and click and treat good responses or offer the promise of a toy to play with.

It is extremely important to be patient with a dog whilst retraining is in progress. Post-event castigation will only increase his distress and may promote false competition. Removing faeces after a dog defecates (within sight of the dog) will create an unintended element of competition, which an owner must try to avoid (not always easy in outdoor situations).

Under supervision (in situations when the behaviour is likely to be shown), use the clicker if a dog defecates (to increase reward), and keep his attention by continuing to click and treat. Encourage the dog to walk away from the faeces. Outdoors on streets or pathways, where is it often necessary to pick up faeces in the presence of the dog, offer him a strong chew to be used as a distraction before removal.

Noise Sensitivity and Phobia

German Shepherd Dogs that are 'generally nervous' or neurotic (a condition that ranges from mild to acute) can develop a fear of unusual noises or loud bangs. This nervous condition often worsens (it is progressive) unless it is treated.

Certain sounds can be extremely threatening to a nervous dog and will often trigger a panic response. Thunder and fireworks phobia is common. Once a fear develops, a disturbed dog is often triggered into a wide set of adrenalin-driven behaviours. These range from the flight response – running away in a panic, hiding under furniture and being destructive (attempting to escape) – to inappropriate urination and defecation.

Canine noise phobias originate in nervousness and negative associations. Difficult experiences related to sound, such as exposure to loud fireworks, cars backfiring or industrial-type noises, can have a significant effect on some dogs. Once a negative association with the sound has been formed (when the feared sound occurs in a walk or home area) it can be difficult to change that connection in a dog's mind.

Sound association can work the opposite way with dogs that are not nervous. A good example of this can be seen when gundogs quickly become desensitized to loud bangs during hunting of game. This is because they have made a positive association with the loud noises, especially when they are enjoying working or training.

Noise sensitivity cannot be overcome by excessive petting and stroking or by offering excessive concerned attention. This 'human' caring response will often make matters far worse by reinforcing or supporting the dog's distress. It may even suggest to a dog that the owner is also frightened or disturbed and made anxious by the sound that is feared.

Methods used in the treatment of human phobias, such as exposure therapy or flooding (continually exposing the phobia sufferer to that which is feared) have not achieved success when used in the treatment of dogs. It is not possible to desensitize a dog in this manner because he cannot be counselled. In my clinical case files, it has been proved that the more a nervous dog is exposed to the situation that is feared, the more likely he will be to display the flight response.

Treatment should instead be aimed at making a dog more secure with the owner and his environment. The best method of retraining a dog is through desensitization: reducing noise sensitivity and counter-conditioning (interruption and reward). The playing of recordings of feared sounds, unless coupled with behavioural therapy, will

Some nervous or hyper-alert dogs may react adversely to visual and audible stimuli.

serve only to reinforce the fear association and make the dog more frightened.

Distraction and Positive Reinforcement

In all but the truly acute cases it should be possible to use an established sound and reward method to attract a dog's attention and distract him from the sound perceived to be a threat. In our clinic sessions we practise using the sound of a reward whistle when a dog is displaying nervousness. The dog is then called and offered a significant reward (food, a novel toy for retrieval play, or a walk) together with a Sit instruction. All good responses are clicker signalled and rewarded. Providing that the sound signal has already been established – linked with a reward – a dog should begin to develop some 'attention conflict' between fear of the sound and the lure of the reward. A significant food reward, such as fatty mince or dried cooked liver, should be used.

The onset of nervous behaviour can be interrupted by standing in another room and using the reward whistle system to switch the dog's attention. However, for this, the sound must have been linked to reward, and it must have been used randomly for at least seven to fourteen days around the home so that the dog will not associate the system with the feared noise.

A short, rewarded, retrieval play session with a special toy, or a Control Walk session, can be diverting to a nervous dog, and this method has proved successful in many cases. Over a period of an hour or two, create several five-minute well-rewarded sessions, followed by rest periods. The ideal retrieval item is a dumb-bell, training dummy or a soft ball. Avoid any challenge and adrenalin-driven 'excitement' that can stimulate hyper-activity and also hyper-alertness.

It is important to have continual sounds around a dog in the home. If possible, leave a talk-radio programme playing in the background (gradually raise the volume) and randomly (and discretely) make available durable chews, uncooked bones or foraging or treat-ball toys to distract the dog and help to reduce hyper-alertness.

Once some level of behavioural improvement has been made with a nervous dog it should be possible to introduce special sessions to help deal with the condition. For distraction and interruption methods to be successful a controlled scenario is needed: work on a random indoor recall session while a hidden helper creates a 'noise' (not too loud or frightening to begin with!).

The controlled scenario in the home has several advantages over a 'real' event in that participants can be both alert and prepared. A created noise can be both timed and volume-controlled and the dog should benefit from an owner being able to offer complete atten-

tion. Repeated sessions can in the long term desensitize a dog to noises and mean appropriate behaviour can be rewarded and promoted. A dog is normally more confident in the home than outdoors, and this factor can help in the treatment of noise phobia.

It is best to take this procedure extremely slowly. As discussed previously, it is counter-productive to over-expose a dog to any noises feared as this can make the condition progressive and create an acute phobic response.

If real progress is being made then a dog may be exposed to low sound-level recording of noises, fireworks or thunder during special controlled play sessions (*see* clicker- and reward-whistle training) in order to promote a subconscious positive association.

The use of a folding travel crates, with a cover, will create the den effect and help a nervous dog to feel protected and secure.

A Support Dog

It may be possible to use another dog as a canine mentor to promote change in a nervous dog's behaviour. If another dog shows no interest in the feared noise, object or situation then the nervous dog may begin to consider it less of a threat. It is essential that the support dog is calm and non-aggressive and has proved not to react fearfully to the types of sounds used in a controlled scenario. The dogs should first be socialized together on a walk in a novel field or walk area.

Realistic Expectations

Desensitizing any dog to a phobia or a nervous 'fear' condition that has developed over time is not straightforward and will probably require much patience on the part of all family members.

The retraining sessions (the controlled scenario) should be repeated as many times as possible so that you establish a connection between the feared sounds, calmness, and reward. In the short term (the first month or two), a dog being desensitized to feared noises may make seemingly insignificant steps towards recovery. However, these small steps of progress are critical in that they show the first signs to a change in behaviour that will have been reinforced over a period. In the long term (three to six months), a dog's insecurity should be treated.

Vehicle- and travel-associated problem behaviours

During a vehicle journey, neurotic or nervous behaviours may occur when a dog is distressed and fearful or he reacts excitedly or adversely to stimuli. Such a dog can show signs of sickness, acute hyperactivity, aggressiveness and general restlessness.

The range of inappropriate behaviours displayed by some dogs may be rooted in, or triggered by, a number of factors. In my clinical cases nervous dogs have made a negative association when travelling in a car. This association could be as a result of an early visit to the vet, when a traumatic event – such as an injection, handling by a stranger, aggression from other dogs – may have occurred. In rescue and re-homed dogs, there may already be a negative association with car journeys. The cause of this may range from rejection, capture, being a stray and the associated trauma of navigating busy roads.

The other various influencing aspects of car-specific dog behaviour include a need to display protective and territorial aggression towards any perceived threat to the car and its occupants, neurotic insecurity (general canine nervousness), learned behaviour or faulty learning, confinement and early trauma. There can also be over-interest in surroundings, which can lead to hyper-alertness because of the potential anticipation and excitement that is related to car journeys. Many dogs enjoy their favourite walk (hunting and foraging) to the beach or woodlands in association with a vehicle journey, and the almost numerous behavioural cues (coat, lead, keys, hat, change of shoes, and so on) that precede such a journey, together with the time taken to reach the destination, may trigger ongoing car hyperactivity in some dogs.

If a dog reacts fearfully to a vehicle journey – excessive panting and slavering, trembling, whining or even refusing to enter the vehicle – it indicates that the experience is distressing and that a true phobia has developed. In some cases a dog may display fear-aggression that can be directed towards owners, other dogs and strangers. These behaviours are usually based on one or more traumatic early experiences and can be compounded by strong- willed or dominant dogs. It is essential to identify the stimuli that trigger the inappropriate behaviour.

As with the noise phobias, you may be able to promote a change in a dog's behaviour by having him accompanied by another dog who is calm and confident in the car. If this role-model dog shows no interest in the feared event then the fearful dog may consider car journeys less stressful. However, in some cases, the second dog can pick up the nervousness and hyperactivity and then the problem is doubled.

Retraining
When beginning a programme of desensitization, the best results are gained by taking each step as slowly as possible. It is advisable to gently repeat each stage, especially the early steps.

It is best to start the retraining programme with the vehicle parked in the home drive or close by. Place a travel crate into the back of the vehicle. Then, following a very short Control Walk, calmly commence cleaning the seats whilst the vehicle doors are open and the dog is in attendance. Repeatedly click and treat the dog as he approaches or explores the area around the car. Sometimes sit in the vehicle without the engine running and wipe down the windows and the dashboard with a cloth.

Now attempt to encourage the dog to enter. However, it is vital that you do not press the issue as this will only make the dog more anxious. Leave the doors and tailgate open. This 'opening session' can last as long as required. Finish this first stage of the programme with a well-rewarded click and treated Control Walk. Always attempt to finish on a positive note. Return the crate from the car to the home.

The Journey

Once the dog will enter the car, ideally straight into the travel crate, you can attempt a journey. It is important to remain as calm as possible during a car journey to prevent the dog from being aroused by any abnormal behaviour on your part. Anxious or apprehensive behaviour shown by you or passengers will be directly transmitted to the dog, and it is known that most problem behaviours can be reinforced by human nervousness and apprehension.

It is vital to the success of the strategy that the dog's movements within the car are as restricted as possible. The use of a covered dog crate will restrict movement and, perhaps more importantly, have a calming effect on the nervous dog. The added benefit of a travel crate is that it reduces the range of potential stimuli.

On a short journey, stop the vehicle. You or a fellow passenger, should 'confidently' step out and walk around. If the dog has remained calm, re-enter the vehicle and continue. Praise (click and treat) any appropriate behaviour. If distress or hyperactivity is shown, bring the dog out of the vehicle for a five-minute clicker-rewarded Control Walk. Go back to the vehicle with the minimum of fuss and return home.

Make random short vehicle journeys that are not associated with walks or repetitive trips such as those to the supermarket, to see relatives and so on. You can then make a journey to a favourite walk area.

If the dog becomes distressed or over-excited at any of these stages it is always advisable to end the session. Always attempt to find a positive behaviour to reward at the end of the session. This may be shown when the back of the vehicle is opened or when the dog is made to sit upon leaving the vehicle. If a display of acute hyperactivity occurs during the short journey, attempt to reduce the behaviour by saying 'No' while using training discs to signal non-reward.

At each positive step you must praise the dog for any appropriate behaviour and any success. Do not react to any inappropriate behaviour except to say 'No' calmly and to signal with the training discs.

If the dog is over-stimulated by the outside surroundings, he will feel psychologically rewarded by the movement of the vehicle. Shield his vision with the strategic placing of blinds, and withdraw the perceived reward by stopping whenever necessary.

The behavioural therapy process requires much patience, especially in the early stages. Over a period of time, you will need to keep repeating journey procedures – entering the car, switching ignition on, moving away – until your dog becomes desensitized.

Road- and Traffic-related Phobias and Excitability

German Shepherd Dogs that have not experienced urban traffic, those that have suffered difficult experiences associated with road traffic, and those that have been socialized only in rural areas, are the most like to suffer from road phobia. As with treating noise phobia, methods used in the treatment of human phobias – such as continually exposing the phobia sufferer to that which is feared – have not achieved success when used on dogs.

The best method of retraining a road-nervous dog is through reward conditioning. If a dog can be brought under better control through a training regime (especially one that conditions acceptable responses, such as the clicker system) then it is possible to desensitized the dog. Clicker training has proved extremely helpful in my clinical cases. However, during initial retraining, the reward must be significant – small pieces of blanched raw, fatty mince or liver cake.

Commence the retraining during a time when traffic is relatively light: at a weekend or on in the mid-afternoon. Before you begin the training session, it is strongly advisable to undertake a Control Walk away from the main road, using a short, uncomplicated, webbing, or leather, lead and a head-control collar.

1. When you are ready, move near to the route where the dog is displaying the problem behaviours. If the dog pulls or attempts to move to one side during this part of the walk, attract his attention with the sound of the reward whistle or show a favourite toy.

2. Once you have the dog's attention, instruct him to sit, and reward obedience. If any acute signs of nervous behaviour are shown these should be signalled with the training discs and the session should be broken off. If the dog has shown a good response and is under control (little or no excitability or pulling behaviour shown), continue the Control Walk towards the feared route. Go part way and then return home. Repeat this step over several days.

3. Set up a scenario in which a friend and a child approach the dog during the walk. During the session it is essential that everyone remains calm and relaxed (and in possession of a clicker and dog treats). They should approach, instruct him to sit and they should also offer a click and reward once the initial greeting has been made and the dog has been instructed to sit once more.

Following success with this event everyone must then ignore the dog. This reduction in attention should be continued during the journey home. Once the dog has been released from the lead, the dog should be placed in his den – if a crate or indoor kennel is used – and left there for at least 15 minutes in order to relax. Repeat this stage several times over a period of weeks rather than days.

4. Continue the retraining at a quiet time. Give the dog a Control Walk on or close to the feared route, clicker signalling the various instructions. It is vital that the dog is not permitted to pull (which is the dog trying to lead). Always give the instruction to sit, which is both passive and boring, so that the dog understands that pulling will not gain him an advantage whereas obedience equals progress.

Over a period of several weeks change the times when a Control Walk is given to the dog on the feared route to include periods when traffic levels have increased. The more gradual this exposure to the feared route, the better.

As with the other phobias discussed in this chapter, desensitizing a dog to a road-traffic phobia is not easy and will require much patience on the part of all the owner and family members. It requires that the process sequence ir repeated as many times as possible until, eventually, the nervous dog begins to make the connection between the feared location and the reward, and as a result develops more positive associations.

Tail chewing and chasing behaviours are canine signs of stress and poor socialization. They should be dealt with carefully because of the addictive nature of the obsessive-compulsive condition.

Obsessive-compulsive Behaviour

Dogs that are nervous or neurotic may develop obsessive and compulsive disorder-like conditions (OCDs), which are characterized by the repetitive or ritual performance of neurotic behaviours (stereotypical behaviour), such as tail-chasing, excessive grooming (licking), circling, moving from side to side repeatedly, air gulping, continual door scratching and obsessive chewing (to name a few). In acute cases, the behaviours can include inappropriate urination and defecation, destructiveness and even collapse. Some OCD behaviours may direct a dog hyperactively towards moving or stationary targets such as shadows, reflective lights and sounds (the telephone ringing, and so on). These actions are all 'stress-related' behaviours.

OCDs are self-rewarding in that as the behaviour is performed, the brain produces

This and the two pictures opposite clearly illustrate a young German Shepherd 'patient' (whose owner adopted him from another family member) that has developed the stress-related obsessive and compulsive condition of tail-chasing and biting. The display showed that the condition had become acute, and was extremely distressing to watch.

At this point, the OCD behaviour means that the dog cannot respond to his adopted owner in any way. It is so extreme that the imbalance in the dog's brain chemistry distorts his perception, and he can no longer control his physical movements.

In this picture the dog has his tail outstretched as he is driven to chase it in a display of manic behaviour that is sometimes associated with the condition.

Unlike humans, dogs have three eyelids. The upper and lower eyelids share ducts that drain away moisture, while the third eyelid, which is visible as a pale membrane across the inside corner of the eye, helps to clean the eye's surface. The third eyelid is naturally more developed – and therefore more obvious – in some breeds than it is in others: this is not a cause for concern.

Ears, Eyes and Nose

Examine the ears for signs of mites (*see* page 111), soreness or excessive dirt. The outer ear can be safely cleaned from the inner to the outer regions with a cotton-wool ball partly soaked in slightly warmed water. (Use a clean piece of cotton wool for each ear.) Regular cleaning will usually prevent most bacterial infections from taking hold and becoming acute and therefore much more difficult to treat. It is possible to use a dropper to introduce cleaning oil that can be massaged into the ear and cleaned out.

If a dog appears to have mucus or a wet area beneath any eye, wipe it gently with a damp cotton wipe. (Cotton wool should not be used because the fine strands can be left behind in the eye.) Always wipe away from the eyes and the tear ducts, and ensure that the cotton wipe is rinsed clean before wiping again. As with the ears, use a fresh cotton wipe for the other eye. The eye can also be flushed with a diluted eye cleaner (*see* page 119).

A dog's nose is kept moist by a special secretion: the dampness enhances the dog's ability to detect new smells. If a puppy or dog has a damp nose it is thought by many people to be an indication that the animal is in good health. However, not all dogs (or breeds) have a distinctly damp nose so, once again, knowing your dog well will enable you to judge whether the condition of the nose is normal. If your dog has an exceptionally dry nose, it is worth having the dog examined by the vet.

Any excessive discharge from the eyes or nose should immediately alert an owner to health concerns. This also applies to any blackness or inflammation within the ears.

Skin, Coat and Paws

One of the easiest guides to the general health of a dog is the overall appearance of the coat. A coat that is unusually coarse, dry, greasy or staring can indicate any number of general health problems, not just skin conditions. Dogs naturally lose hair through moulting, but any localized hair loss may indicate a skin condition, such as eczema, or parasite infestation, such as mange. Soiling around the anal area is also cause for concern. Regular grooming and health inspections will alert you to any such problems. Skin disorders should always be discussed with a veterinary surgeon. The sooner a problem is correctly identified, the easier it will be to treat.

Make a habit of checking your dog's pads for any foreign bodies. Since the German Shepherd does not have long silky hair, debris does not tend to become trapped in the hair surrounding the pads. However, the odd thorn or similar may penetrate the areas between the pads. Any such foreign bodies should be carefully removed (*see* page 118).

Get into the habit of giving your dog a weekly health check: inspect the eyes, ears and mouth, and the coat and paws. This routine need not be too time-consuming, although this will of course depend on how many German Shepherds you have!

Grooming

Most books recommend that an adult dog should be groomed about two or three times a week, but I doubt this advice is followed through by complacent owners. The amount of grooming a dog requires is dictated by the type of walks (whether these are in fields and forests or on urban streets), and the type of coat (a short-haired German Shepherd requires less brushing than a long-haired one). In either case, regular attention to the coat will certainly prevent matting and reduce natural hair loss in the home.

Before you start a grooming session, have any equipment, such as grooming brush, comb and cotton wipes – as well as treats – ready. Then call your dog. With a dog that is excited by grooming, offer a food treat (signalled by the clicker) for responding correctly. If your German Shepherd is long-haired, pay particular attention to the armpits, behind the ears, and the 'trousers' on the hind legs as these areas are especially prone to becoming matted.

Rewards can be continually offered for good behaviour during the session. Make grooming as brief as possible if your dog's dignity appears to be challenged. Some dogs drool when being groomed. Sometimes it depends on who is doing the grooming!

Bath Time

Frequent bathing should be avoided as the shampoo removes the natural oils that are necessary to protect your dog from the cold and wet. However, you may on occasion need to bath or shower your dog, especially after a delicious walk across muddy fields and woodlands. If your dog makes a frequent habit of getting muddy, you can rinse him off without shampoo, or you can brush away the mud when it dries. In any case, it is wise to accustom a puppy to the routine of bathing as early as possible.

To give your dog a bath you will need a shampoo specially made for use on dogs. There is a whole range of different shampoos available, but unless your dog has a particular skin condition (in which case you will require veterinary advice) it is best to stick to the basic ones that do not contain excessive amounts of perfume. Before you start, partially fill the bath with lukewarm water. If your dog loves having a bath it is best not to run the hot water before the cool because, if you are distracted, there is always the chance that he will leap straight into the water and scald himself. Have several towels available in anticipation of the obligatory shaking behaviour. Think of the pre-bathing procedure as a military-style operation with as much as possible prepared in advance but as little visible build-up as possible to avoid causing your dog to become nervous or over-excited.

When everything is ready, put your dog on a short lead (especially if he is likely to bound about during the washing procedure) and lift him into the bath. Fully soak your dog's coat and underbelly using a large sponge. If you use a shower head, make sure the water is not hot (test it with the back of your hand) before spraying your dog with it. Then quickly apply the shampoo. Do not use too much shampoo: use as little as possible – no more than is necessary to produce a lather – to minimize removal of the natural oils.

Then rinse thoroughly with buckets of fresh water or the shower head. Be very particular about removing all residues of sham-

poo as any that remains in the coat can cause irritation. Always ensure that the water temperature is not too hot. When the coat is completely rinsed – the water will run clear – squeeze out any excess water with your hands. This is when you'll need the towels ready because your dog will want to have a good shake. Use the towels to dry him off as well as possible.

Diet and Feeding

A healthy diet will offer a dog the ideal balance between protein and bulk together with all the vitamins and minerals needed for a healthy life. The best diets are probably the complete, dry foods because as well as being specially formulated to provide the dog with all his nutritional requirements, they are very convenient to use.

It is especially important that puppies and young dogs are given a balanced diet, ideally one that is formulated for growing dogs. Nowadays, most dog-food manufacturers produce a range of foods to suit dogs of different ages and activity levels, so owners need not be concerned about having to make adjustments to meet their individual dog's requirements. Sometimes it is tempting to offer little extras such as fresh steamed vegetables or fresh meat to break the routine and make the meal more palatable. However, most dogs are not nearly as fussy as we are, and such additions serve little useful purpose and may in fact cause problems in that they can give rise to looseness and even diarrhoea. Extras are better given in the form of treats (*see* liver recipe, Chapter 4, page 46). Nutritional advice on feeding dogs varies, and there are many conflicting opinions. However, it is generally wise to avoid snack foods or treats that are known to cause problems (*see* box right).

Your dog will appreciate a proper feeding routine. If the feeding time varies from day to day, an insecure dog may feel anxious. So establish a feeding time that is convenient and then stick to it. A short while after the main walk is a good time. Most mature dogs are fed once a day, but there is good argument for dividing up the daily ration into a small breakfast and an afternoon/evening meal so that he can eat twice a day, especially if your dog is a highly exercised, hearty eater. Young puppies, of course, require an altogether different routine in that they need to be fed little and often.

Parasites

There are various types of parasite – internal and external – that use dogs as hosts. However, most can be prevented with simple precautions.

The most common internal parasites are tapeworms and roundworms, which cause a range of problems, including weight loss, and can be extremely debilitating. Roundworm often causes the most concern because of the very small risk of its being passed to humans. Roundworm lies dormant in adult dogs, but is reactivated in pregnancy. Puppies are therefore born carrying worms because the larvae migrate through the placenta or via the mother's milk. Tapeworm eggs are carried by fleas. Dogs may ingest fleas when biting at themselves to relieve irritation caused by flea bites. This is one of the many reasons why flea control is important.

In the warmer months of the year, all dogs and puppies are likely to pick up fleas, especially if they come into contact with other animals or visit other houses. Excessive scratching is the most obvious sign of infestation. Some dogs are especially allergic to flea bites: in such cases the skin becomes exceptionally itchy and inflamed, giving rise to skin infection.

The ticks that affect dogs are usually deer or sheep ticks, so they are usually picked up

---

Snacks and treats to avoid

- Chocolate intended for human consumption (it contains a potentially deadly ingredient, theobromine).
- Excessive amounts of lean cooked or processed meat.
- Crisps and similar salty snacks.
- Cheese.

Of these foods, the high-protein ones especially can create digestive imbalance. This in turn may lead to loose bowels and hyperactivity or hyper-alertness. For dogs that have sensitive skin and are prone to itchiness, dairy products and offal should be avoided.

---

in the countryside from pasture used to graze farm animals or in areas where there is a deer population. These spider-like parasites climb on to their host, usually making their way to the head and neck area. They then attach themselves to the skin and feed on the animal's blood. To obtain their fill they remain there for a number of hours, and sometimes for a couple of days. Once attached to the skin and engorged with blood, they look like dark pea-sized warts. They then drop off into the environment. Ticks do not appear to cause the irritation associated with fleas, but they are unpleasant and they do carry diseases that can be transmitted to the dog. Numerous ticks attacking an animal can cause general illness and debility.

There are many types of mite, which cause a variety of conditions ranging from the minor to the very serious. Ear mites are fairly common microscopic creatures that live in the ear canal, especially in puppies. They cause inflammation and itchiness, and the production of excessive wax which is apparent as black sludge or specks. Harvest mites can also cause intense irritation. They are picked up in late summer, when the larvae crawl on to the feet, legs and belly of the

Countryside walks and health risks

It is important to be wary of exposing any dog to extremes of terrain and to potential contact with dogs or other animals that may be carrying diseases or harbouring parasites such as fleas, mites and ticks.

After a countryside walk, where both dog and owner have been exposed to areas where livestock is grazing, or where there is bracken or stream water, it is advisable to bath the dog (as well as taking a shower yourself). After bathing, be sure to dry the dog thoroughly and then give him a good grooming session. Once he is clean, it should be easier to check him for any cuts, ticks, fleas, and so on, and deal with them quickly.

It may go without saying that an owner should be confident of 100 per cent recall before releasing a dog onto open moors or the more remote countryside areas where livestock may be grazing. Quite aside from the need to avoid alarming the animals, sheep and cattle can be a source of a number of infections and parasites that can be transmitted to dogs.

host. Other kinds of mite cause different types of mange, some of which can be very serious.

Treatment and Prevention

It is absolutely essential to worm your puppy or dog regularly. Apart from causing illness and debility in the dog, some worms can infect humans. A puppy should be wormed frequently until he is six months old; thereafter he can be wormed as for adult dogs: every three months. Treatments for tapeworm can be given to an adult dog every three to six months. The worming preparations available today are highly effective and simple to use, so there should be no need for a dog to become infested with worms. A veterinary nurse will be pleased to offer helpful information on the range of treatments.

Fleas can be prevented by regular use of specially formulated insecticides, which are available in a variety of forms: spray, shampoo, and the modern 'spot-ons', which are applied via a pipette onto the dog's neck. You can also use insecticidal collars. Some of these preventative measures are wide-ranging in their effect so they are effective against both ticks and fleas. Ear mites must be treated with a parasiticide prescribed by your vet. They are passed easily from dog to dog (and to cats), so all dogs and cats in your household should be treated at the same time.

Some treatments are injected or given orally in tablet form, but these must of course be obtained from the vet. The best treatments will help eradicate all the commonly encountered, external parasites.

When dealing with fleas, bear in mind that the flea breeds in the environment, not on your dog, so treating your dog will not destroy the eggs. It is therefore important to treat the dog's bed, any soft furnishings, skirting boards, and carpet, with an insecticide designed for this purpose. (Do not use this environmental spray directly on the animal.) All other pets in the household should also be treated at the same time to prevent cross-infestation.

Ticks can be treated directly with the use of an anti-tick spray. Each individual tick can then be carefully removed with a tick hook (available from a surgery or pet shop) or it can be allowed to fall off. Do not just pull the tick out of a dog's skin because the head may break off and remain under the skin where it can cause an abscess to form.

Most flea, tick and mite treatments will protect a dog for between one and six months. Ideally they should be given in spring and late summer or early autumn because it is during the warmer months that these parasites are most active. However, it is worth considering that central heating may extend the breeding season for fleas, so treatment in winter may also be necessary.

Signs of Ill Health

A dog that is in good health will have bright eyes, a damp nose, a glossy or neat coat, sweet breath, lively trot, wagging tail and pricked-up ears. Any change in a German Shepherd Dog's normal appearance should alert an owner to the existence of a health problem. The first signs of a limp, any bouts of abnormal panting, continual vomiting or diarrhoea, or excessive whining, are fairly straightforward physical signs of ill health. But there are also behavioural signs, which might include a reduction in the normal enthusiasm for walks, general listlessness, loss of appetite, excessive water intake, and so on. Behavioural signs may be very subtle, detectable only by an alert owner who will notice that on returning home the dog's greeting is a little subdued, or that on retrieving his favourite ball he doesn't seem to have quite as much energy as usual. As the relationship between dog and owner develops, the owner will be able to detect the slight changes in personality and behaviour. Any such signs may indicate a problem.

The normal patterns of activity at the puppy stage – playing, chewing and exploring, eating, toileting and sleeping – will confirm the puppy is on a happy and healthy development cycle. Puppies change quickly, so temporary changes in activity or feeding and sleep patterns should not always be a cause for alarm. However, if there is a dramatic or lasting change, a health check is advisable.

Ongoing diarrhoea, vomiting or sudden weight loss should be treated very seriously. Consult your veterinary surgeon as quickly as possible.

Anal Glands

The correlation between a dog's behaviour and his physical condition can be both acute and not immediately obvious. One example that would serve to illustrate this arose during

---

Diarrhoea

The causes of diarrhoea are varied. They range from dietary change (either introduced by the owner or resulting from scavenging) to bacterial infections and potentially fatal diseases.

Whatever the cause, diarrhoea can in itself be very serious because repeated bouts give rise to dehydration, which, in puppies especially, can be severe and ultimately life-threatening. Ongoing diarrhoea should always be investigated by the vet. A short bout may simply be a reaction to a change in the dog's diet or environment and may be nothing to worry about providing the situation is closely monitored. However, if you are in any doubt at all, take the animal to the vet.

It can take some time for a young puppy to fight off the debilitating effects of an intestinal infection. The use of antibiotic treatment will often reduce the natural bacteria that are required by a dog's digestive system to break down foods. Some foods can compensate for the loss of a biological balance in a puppy's system. A veterinary surgeon or nurse will be only too pleased to discuss food types.

Adult dogs that show signs of long-term looseness or diarrhoea, but that are otherwise healthy, may require a change in diet. Older, less active, dogs do not require high-protein foods, and they may benefit from changing to one of the low-protein foods that are available at good pet shops or veterinary clinics.

---

the very early days of my clinic, when I came across a number of dogs with anal gland infection or impaction. It didn't take long for me to make a tentative correlation between nervous male dogs and some sort of anal gland problem. Because of my suspicions, I began to include questions about anal gland conditions in the diagnostic questionnaire that is given to all prospective clients to complete before we commence treatment.

The research books relating to dogs in nature suggest that the anal gland is fully operational only in canines in the wild. In these canines, the anal gland is used to add an extra scent marker on to faeces and on to

This picture of Rocky clearly illustrates his dedication to Amanda. As a 'pet shop puppy' and the subject of adoption, he displayed almost all the canine behavioural-disorder signs that it is possible to predict. Although nervous and insecure, Rocky responded positively to my treatment and to all the care and affection from his owner.

grass and low bushes. However, my hypothesis is that in domesticated dogs, especially those that are insecure, the gland is probably stimulated by neural messages that respond to the dog's need to mark a territory to make it secure. The anal gland in the dog may be on a par with our appendix: this part of human anatomy is no longer of any practical use since it was originally designed to cope with primitive man's different diet.

My interest in the connection between nervous domesticated dogs and impacted anal glands was prompted by the number of

dogs in my clinic that were displaying the condition. I began to investigate two, long-term, cases involving a GSD/Collie crossbreed called Rocky, and a Miniature Poodle named Cadeu. In these cases I was extremely fortunate to be able to maintain regular contact with the clients over several years, which proved essential in developing my basic understanding of the condition.

The first dog, Rocky, belonged to Amanda, who bought him from a pet shop when he was ten weeks old. Apparently, the puppy had previously been sold to another

A nervous GSD is rarely off guard. He will keep his eyes open and his ears in the upright, alert position, continually listening for any sounds and watching for any events or movements that his neurosis makes him think he needs to worry about.

family who after two weeks had returned him and demanded a refund because he was too difficult to handle.

In the early days, Amanda felt Rocky was a little bit more mischievous than normal but because of his relatively small size as a puppy his problem behaviours were manageable. Rocky and Amanda were soon devoted to each other and very quickly became inseparable. Rocky would even follow her to the bathroom.

At about six months of age Rocky developed destructive behaviour (Separation-related Disorder), and this was problematic because by now he was large enough to cause considerable damage in her home. He had managed to wreck her double bed in one afternoon, and he had also destroyed her carpets, a three-piece suite, scratched his way through doors and generally wreaked havoc. When Rocky was 12 months old Amanda moved house. The new home was in a rural location and had a conservatory with a tiled floor. This room was used to isolate him and contain the amount of damage he could do.

Some time later, Amanda's partner left and Rocky become even more attached to her. He was becoming increasingly anxious and agitated in her presence as well as in her absence. Amanda moved yet again to be nearer to her job. The new house didn't have a conservatory and Rocky had to be left with the run of the house. She had shut him out of her bedroom and the lounge in a bid to minimize the damage he could do, but it soon became apparent that this strategy was far from satisfactory. Rocky continued to damage carpets and doors in a bid to access her when she left him alone in the home. He also developed a habit of swinging on curtains until the rail gave way.

At roughly the same time, Rocky developed what Amanda referred to as 'a problem with his bottom', and this seemed to be causing him some pain. He would continually adopt a sitting position and then drag himself forward with his forelegs so that his bottom rubbed along the floor. He had also developed a lick granuloma from stress-related excessive self-grooming.

Previously, Rocky had been extremely disruptive during visits to the veterinary surgery. Having moved to a new area and registered with a new vet, Amanda made an

Signs that indicate a visit to the vet

Not all of the following conditions are emergencies. However, all should be investigated by a vet, in some cases immediately. Any abnormal breathing or bleeding from a large wound, the mouth, nose, genitals or anus should be included in the important signs that indicate an emergency visit to the vet. General loss of condition, such as a dull or staring coat, should also be investigated. An examination by a vet may involve a temperature check, a blood test, an antibiotic injection, or emergency treatment.

Intestinal infections
- Diarrhoea (loose faeces for more than a day)
- Discoloured or blood-stained faeces
- Weight loss
- Vomiting

External parasite infestation or dermatological allergy
- Excessive scratching
- Baldness

Internal parasite infestation
- Weight loss
- Staring coat; loss of condition
- Vomiting (when infestation severe)

Eye infections (such as conjunctivitis) and glaucoma
- Discharge
- Inflammation, redness or swelling

- Blocked tear ducts
- Grey coating and cataracts
- Third eyelid exposed (in some breeds this is normal)

Major organ disease, or diabetes, or stress
- Excessive drinking of water
- Listlessness
- Loss of appetite
- Weight loss
- Eye discolouring

Seizure, heart disease or airway blockage
- Convulsions
- Excessive coughing
- Collapse

Poisioning
- Vomiting
- Convulsions
- Excessive coughing
- Staggering gait; collapse

Joint or muscle problems
- Inflammation, redness or swelling around the joints
- An awkward gait or distinctive limp
- Refusal or hesitation to jump onto a step, over a stile, or into a vehicle
- Yelping when the joint or legs are touched during grooming or wiping down

appointment to discuss the problems. Rocky, true to form, raced into the examining room, knocked the table flying and all the instruments off the trolley. The vet, not surprisingly, was clearly disturbed by his behaviour but nonetheless gave Rocky a thorough examination and eventually identified impacted anal glands.

The veterinary then emptied the anal glands and advised Amanda to bring him back if the problem recurred. Six weeks later, the two of them were back in the surgery with the same problem. However, by that time, Amanda had reached what she referred to as 'a very painful decision'. Rocky and she would finally have to part as she was then on the edge of despair and just couldn't allow him to continue expensively wrecking her home. In addition, she had observed that Rocky was clearly unhappy and very distressed. In an interview on my website, Amanda has recalled sitting in the vet's consulting room, sobbing and trying to explain to the vet that whilst Rocky meant the world to her she couldn't carry on with him as he was. Rocky was, during that time, pacing around the room squeaking and pausing only to chew and lick his feet.

The vet said he could see that Rocky had developed a chronic anxiety problem in addition to his lick-granuloma and the anal-gland disorder. He went on to explain that he would fully understand if Amanda decided to have the dog 'put to sleep' but said that she could try one last solution: he referred Rocky to me. The rest is history on my website. Within three months Rocky responded wonderfully to treatment: with every month, he became calmer, and he no longer displayed the destructive signs of SRD. The next hurdle for him to overcome was an operation to remove his anal glands. I explained to Amanda that following the operation, one of the keys to his successful treatment was to remain perfectly calm and relaxed in Rocky's presence and not to show any signs of panic or concern for his condition. The expected post-operative trauma did not occur.

However, even though Rocky had had his anal glands removed, in the months that followed he would still on occasions rub his bottom along the floor as though it still irritated him. In discussions with Amanda I hypothesized that Rocky's bottom-rubbing behaviour might not be so different from the experience of amputee humans who continue to have sensations in their absent arm or leg. However, the clue to the cause of the behaviour came in the next trauma a year later when Rocky experienced a scare at a local boarding kennel. Once home he started to drag his bottom again, and it appeared that this had become an attention-seeking mechanism. (I had already successfully treated him for attention-seeking scratching using aversion therapy. This was after he had endured blood tests for every known allergy.) As if to support my theory, the signs of anal irritation ended once Rocky had calmed down again.

In the case of Cadeu, the Miniature Poodle, the owner, Jason, had been shown how to empty the dog's anal glands by a veterinary friend who had re-homed the dog to him. I was eventually referred by a vet to treat the dog for Separation-related Disorder. The dog was 'howling the house' down when left behind, and Jason kindly recorded a CD of the wolf noise for me.

As the treatment progressed Jason found that he had to empty his dog's anal glands less and less frequently. As a friendship developed between Jason and me, I was given the rare opportunity to follow the dog's progress over years rather than months. Long-term access to clinical information helped me research ongoing anal-gland disorder in both dogs.

Following these two cases, I began to encounter more and more dogs with anal-gland conditions, and many of these were German Shepherds and crossbreeds. My hypothesis is that a high ratio of German Shepherds suffer from anal gland conditions because it is a strong, territorial breed.

As I write this book I am still investigating potential links between conditions such as territorial insecurity (fairly common in rescue dogs) and obsessive urine marking alongside anal-gland impaction or infection. I hope one day to publish my research data in the hope that veterinary surgeons will be alerted to the link between anal-gland conditions and behavioural conditions defined by territorial insecurity.

First-aid

While a vet should always be consulted about major injuries or ongoing illness, there are a number of minor ailments or injuries that can easily be treated by the competent dog owner. Some require instant first-aid, even if the dog must then visit the vet for further treatment.

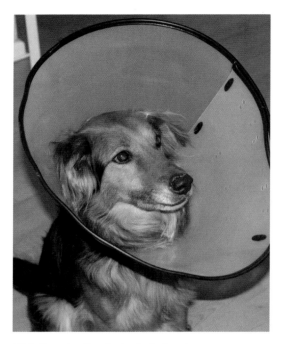

This funnel collar device is designed to prevent a dog from chewing or licking at surgical stitches or areas that have been treated with creams or other substances. These collars are supplied by the vet, but it is possible to make a temporary funnel collar from a circle of cardboard. Added protection can be given to feet by fitting an old sock over the affected foot and securing it with self-adhesive bandage or tape.

Growing and adult German Shepherd Dogs are prone to muscle sprain during over-extended bouts of play or hyperactivity and also during extended walks on agility-testing terrain. For this reason it is important to restrict a growing puppy to controlled periods of exercise and play. The most suitable treatment for a sprain is to immediately apply a cold, cotton, or towel compress to the area twice every hour. This will help reduce swelling. After several applications, the cold compress should be replaced with a warm water compress (which will encourage blood flow to the muscle).

Any cuts, wounds or splinters in the pads or the paws should first be bathed. Splinters of wood or metal in the foot should be carefully removed with tweezers to be confident that all the material has been properly removed. Bathe the area with a mild antiseptic solution to help prevent the likelihood of a secondary infection. Minor cuts and scratches elsewhere on the body can be washed twice daily for a week with cotton wool soaked in a mild antiseptic diluted in warm water. The same can be applied to mild bites from insects or even other dogs. Wasp stings are effectively treated with vinegar, bee stings with bicarbonate of soda.

Minor burns should be immediately doused in ice-cold water. Then you can apply an antiseptic cream. (Use only creams designed for treating burns; grease-based creams will prevent air getting to the skin and delay healing.) Wounds or burns that are anything more than superficial should always be examined and treated by a veterinary surgeon.

Choking in dogs should be dealt with extremely carefully as this is classed as a veterinary emergency. Open the jaws wide to locate the obstruction. Remove it if possible. If not, take the dog to the vet immediately.

Convulsions may be the result of an epileptic seizure. In this instance, the dog should be removed into a quiet, dark area and given time to recover before being taken to the veterinary clinic.

If it is suspected that a dog has come into contact with a poisonous solution, immediately shower him to prevent access to any residue that may have come into contact with the coat, face or limbs. This is important because the dog's natural instinct is to lick off any irritant or pollutant. If a dog has swallowed poison, you must act quickly. However, unless you know for certain what poison the dog has ingested, *do not* make him vomit. Any corrosive substance, such as bleach, should not be vomited as it can severely damage the oesophagus. If you know what the substance is, but are not sure whether to induce vomiting, you can telephone the vet and ask advice about what to do. If you are advised to make the dog vomit, you can use baking soda or warm salty water as an emetic. However, this is useful only if undertaken immediately following the event. In any case, take your dog to the vet.

If a young dog has suffered serious injury or trauma, such as might be sustained in a road-traffic accident, he should be carried to the veterinary clinic or, ideally, moved within a travel crate or carrier. Adult dogs can be carried to the surgery (ideally by two persons) using a blanket to create a temporary stretcher. While nursing a distressed dog, it is important not to fuss as this may add to any confusion or disorientation the dog may be experiencing. Keep the dog in a quiet corner, remain calm, and use a soothing, low-tone voice, to offer reassurance.

Veterinary Clinic Visits

Very few animals appear to enjoy a visit to the veterinary clinic, although the scents and smells of numerous other 'patients' are probably quite exciting to a young puppy. It is always a good idea to transport a dog, especially a puppy or a young dog, in a special carrying box. This will keep him safe, secure and easy to handle whilst you wait your turn.

If you find it difficult to control your dog or puppy in the surgery, leave him in the car and ask a nurse to advise when it is time to see the vet. When you enter the examination room introduce the pet to the veterinary surgeon and explain the problem or query. Sometimes it is useful to write these details down before the visit and use the notes as a reminder during the examination. This is important because, since the dog can't explain it himself, the vet will rely on your information as well as his physical examina-

Administering treatments and medicines

Few, if any, animals (including humans) enjoy taking medicines. To help 'the medicine go down', tablet treatments can effectively be disguised in tasty titbits such as soft meat. Liquid medicines need to be given with an oral syringe: administer the treatment into the side of the mouth directing it to the back of the tongue. A confident helper, holding the dog's head and fixing the body still between the knees, can make this action brisk and without trauma. This is also a good method for applying ear drops and eyes drops because dogs like to squirm free of the tightest grips when it comes to treatment.

To flush out any unwanted objects such as hair or dust from the dog's eyes, use previously boiled (and cooled) or sterilized water, or a human eye-cleaning solution in a cup of lukewarm water. Use a dropper to administer the solution.

Prepare all that is required before any application of treatment is undertaken. A dog may anticipate actions and attempt avoidance. Any nervousness on the part of an owner will trigger nervousness in a dog. For this reason it is best to be detached and unemotional about the procedure. A positive, confident, military-style approach when administering treatments will be rewarded by a quick recovery in a dog. The faster the treatment is given the better. Most dogs will be as pleased as their owners when a difficult procedure is completed and the basic aspects of the human-canine relationship returns to normal.

tion to diagnose the problem. The communication limitations imposed by the inability of dogs to speak is where a close relationship with a pet can be a wonderful advantage. The owner will probably know better than anyone how a dog or puppy is feeling and if there are problems that the veterinary surgeon needs to address.

The veterinary surgeon will usually require the owner to place the dog onto the examination table where it is easier for him to check him over. The vet will probably take the dog's temperature (anally) and look in the eyes and mouth.

Vet Phobia

Some older dogs, especially those that have been rescued or re-homed, can be nervous or even aggressive during visits to the veterinary clinic. It's no wonder when such visits can involve being stabbed in the bottom or the neck by a stranger. It's not unlike the negative association that humans have with dental surgeries. However, with patience and determination – and co-opeation from the surgery staff – you can de-sensitize a nervous dog and help him overcome his phobia of the veterinary surgery. The following is a step-by-step approach to tackling the problem.

1. Confidently walk the dog on a short lead past the veterinary surgery and then return and pass again. Reward all obedience with a food treat. Pre-arrange for a veterinary nurse to come outside and be introduced to the dog. A special food reward should be offered (click and treat). If the dog is showing calm behaviour, go on to Step 2. If not, break off and repeat the process over several visits.

2. Introduce the dog into a quiet surgery waiting area before or after a clinic session. Ask various people from the surgery to approach the dog. They should praise the dog and offer click-and-treat rewards for all appropriate behaviour (sitting, relaxed attitude, and so on). Do not stroke the dog as this can indicate nervousness.

   If possible, ask people who are not surgery staff to repeat the process so that a nervous dog experiences a reasonable mix of people (as well as the various distinctive scents of veterinary staff). This second step should not last longer than five or ten minutes. You should then leave with the dog. Repeat on an everyday basis

to condition the dog to being approachable when there is no possibility of treatment.

3. Return with the dog to the surgery and reward any relaxed behaviour. Then, if it is acceptable to the veterinary clinic, allow the dog to investigate other rooms – especially the examination room – without any examination or treatment being applied.

   Repeat this step several times in a week if possible. Ask if the veterinary surgeon or senior nurse is available at some stage to come outside the surgery to gently but firmly instruct the dog to sit and take a food treat. This request should be made to fit in with the veterinary clinic's schedule.

4. Have the dog enter the surgery and allow a vet to casually examine him briefly. Click and reward any relaxed behaviour with a food treat. You and your dog should then leave without any clinical treatment being undertaken. Repeat several times.

5. Once every stage has been successfully achieved the dog can be taken into the examination room and treated.

Breeding

The following is a brief guide to the bitch's reproductive cycle and breeding. However, it is irresponsible to allow a dog to become pregnant unless the owner is an experienced dog breeder or a professional. Not only is there the worry and costs of raising puppies but there is the ethical responsibility to find each of them a caring home. My advice is to have a bitch neutered after the first season. In the unfortunate event of an accidental mating, the pregnancy can be terminated by the vet within three days of conception.

German Shepherds usually reach sexual maturity between the ages of six and twelve months.

Reproductive Cycle

A bitch'a reproductive cycle lasts approximately six months and has four stages:

Stage 1: Pro-oestrus

The pro-oestrous stage lasts between one and two weeks and is the time in which the bitch usually shows watery vaginal bleeding. This period precedes the fertile phase when mating results in pregnancy.

Stage 2: Oestrus

The oestrous phase normally lasts between four and seven days. In most bitches, the discharge fades in colour, and becomes thicker but less profuse. It is at this time that the female will accept a dog and mate.

Stage 3: Metoestrus

Metoestrus lasts between six and ten weeks. There are no immediate external signs. However, hormone levels are still high following oestrus, so it is during this time that false or phantom pregnancies may occur.

Stage 4: Anoestrus

Anoestrus, which lasts approximately four months, is the period during which there is no hormonal activity.

Pregnancy

In dogs, pregnancy usually lasts for a around 63 days. A veterinary surgeon will usually confirm pregnancy after an examination at around 30 days. A pregnant bitch requires extra food, vitamins and minerals, and she should be given smaller, more frequent meals. There are specially formulated diets available for pregnant and nursing bitches. It is extremely important that she is wormed at specific times during pregnancy as this will help to reduce the activity of roundworm (*see* page 111). A worming regime for the pregnant bitch should be discussed with the vet.

Remy, with the first two of her litter, is lovingly assisted by GSD breeder and show judge Carol. After the third puppy, Remy's contractions ceased, and she had to be transferred to the veterinary surgery in order to undergo a Caesarean section to save the final four puppies.

Remy is seen here 24 hours later with her full complement of seven puppies. While feeding the puppies, she requires a highly nutritious diet and vitamin and mineral supplements.

The six-week-old puppies have been weaned on to moist, solid foods and have grown into a lively and healthy litter of delightful German Shepherds.

About two weeks before the puppies are due to be born, the bitch will need to be provided with a suitable whelping box. The box should be of an adequate size and lined with lots of newspaper and towels and should be positioned in a quiet area of the home.

Whelping

When it is time for a pregnant bitch to give birth she will go through three stages of labour. In the first phase, which can last for several hours, the bitch will become restless and pant a great deal. The second whelping phase is when the babies are born and the bitch experiences muscls contractions that help to push the puppies out. This phase does not normally exceed six hours, although giving birth to large litters can increase this timespan. The third phase is when the placentae (one for each puppy) is discharged from the uterus.

There are usually between four and eight puppies in a litter. Occasionally large litters containing up to 12 puppies occur. The precise number is dependent on the fertility of the sire, and the number of eggs. Following birth, the litter mother licks the puppies clean and continues to perform this task during what is called the reflex period (the first three weeks).

The puppies soon begin to suckle. Newborn puppies rely on their mother to keep them warm, clean and well fed, and for the first 10 to 15 days of life they are both blind and deaf. When they are very young, puppies tend to sleep a great deal. As they grow older they become increasingly active.

Weaning puppies off their mother's milk and introducing them to solid foods is a gradual process. It can begin from the age of three to five weeks, when the mother starts to break off suckling. This is probably to encourage the puppies' independent development and, perhaps, a great deal to do with sharpening claws and teeth. In the wild, only

Pet insurance

One issue that should be included in any discussions on canine health is pet insurance, which has proved itself a boon to pet owners. The number of people who take out insurance for their animals has increased dramatically in the past ten years, and there can be no doubting the wisdom of taking out insurance for a young dog or puppy. It is easy to fall into the rather fatal attraction of not doing so because your previous dogs have all been healthy and not needed major surgery or behavioural treatment. But you can never take your dog's health for granted – however well you care for him – and an unexpected illness that requires expensive treatment can put great strain on the household budget.

However, it is important to know that not all pet insurance schemes are the same. Many cover homeopathic treatment, for example, while others do not. Most companies have a range of policies that offer different levels of cover. It is worth finding one that has a provision for the treatment of behavioural as well as physical treatment. (Some of the cheaper policies will not cover vital behavioural treatment.) The day a claim is required it is wonderful to know that an insurance pet-plan covers all the dog's physical and psychological health needs.

the alpha female breeds, so some pack bitches will act as surrogates. In domestication, the breeder takes over the surrogate role by feeding five meals a day and encouraging the puppies to lap, rather than suck, in preparation for taking solid food. Puppies are usually fully weaned by eight weeks old.

Old Age

The signs of old age in a dog are not too different from those in humans. Some grey whiskers, reduced sparkle in the eyes, some stiff and creaking joints. By the time a German Shepherd has reached seven years of age he is, in human terms, middle-aged, and a dog of ten years is the equivalent of a

Cassie, at 12 years old, is in the 'twilight' of her life. She is happy to play around the younger dogs and pleased to take short walks, but most of her time is spent resting with the adult group.

human 70-year-old. At twelve years he is an octogenarian! Just like his human counterpart, the dog will be slower to react to changes and may be happy just to take it easy and allow the world to pass by.

A dog in middle and older age requires progressively less protein and carbohydrate in his food than does a growing puppy and semi-mature dog. There is no growing to do in old age and much less activity to fuel. Older dogs require fewer, less strenuous walks than younger dogs, and they will be less inclined to play. The daily walk can be reduced to a gentle stroll to the local shops and back. Some dogs age beautifully and appear to be strong and healthy to the last. And there will always be the extrovert dog who still wants to jump over walls and fences and race across fields. However, the price to pay for this extended athleticism may be stiff joints, strained muscles and exhaustion.

Elderly German Shepherds tend to develop aches, rheumatism and arthritis. As mentioned earlier in this book, the breed has a history of limb and osteo (bone) problems.

There will be noticeable reduction in mobility and vitality. It is at this stage when owners start to lift their dog into the car and are happy to allow long, uninterrupted sleeping bouts. However, these aches and pains can make even the most placid dog bad-tempered and grumpy, just as they do with us. It is important to take these factors into consideration when dealing with an elderly dog.

Older dogs tend to seek out warmth and rest more, and they enjoy a little peace and quiet. Once fully into old age a dog will be happiest taking afternoon naps in a sunlit lounge or snoozing by the fire on those wet and windy autumn and winter evenings. So if your home is to be the venue for a party, or your house is brimming full of visitors for a special occasion, then an older dog will usually appreciate the opportunity to hide away in a den (a covered dog crate) or some other place away from the commotion. Find a quiet room, offer one of your old pullovers as a comfort blanket, and leave a talk radio programme playing in the background. This strategy is also excellent for 'troubled times',

Growing old gracefully together: an elderly GSD-cross with Mary, his worldly wise owner, both of whom want nothing more than companionship and a comfortable place to rest.

such as bonfire night and New Year periods when fireworks are continually exploding.

Older dogs still require regular grooming and attention to dental care. They are more likely to suffer tooth decay (usually indicated by bad breath), and this can also make a dog quite grumpy. Humans are never too happy when they have toothache!

Failing Senses

Infirm dogs can also develop deafness and cataract-type blindness. Usually their sense of smell becomes more acute and this compensates for the loss of those senses. Sight signals can easily be developed for deaf dogs. Sound vibrations (such as a foot stamp) can

be used as signals for dogs whose sense of hearing is compromised as these can be detected easily through the floor. There are vibrating collar systems that can be operated by a remote unit. This system can promote recall when sound signals are no longer effective. In the case of partial blindness, the value of sound signals (clicker, whistle and training discs) can take on even greater significance.

Euthanasia

There may come a time when a dog that is struggling to fight off the ravages of old age finds himself progressively unequal to the battle. A veterinary surgeon may be able to advise you on whether it is unkind to allow

Carol and Remy illustrate the mutual joy and contentment that can define the relationship between a healthy and good-natured German Shepherd Dog and a dedicated owner.

an infirm dog to struggle on. However, owners who know their dogs well are probably the best judges – as long as they can assess the situation rationally. Caring owners are attached to their dogs and, for some, any talk of euthanasia is difficult. If you know that your dog has reached a stage when euthanasia is the kindest thing, but find it difficult to contemplate, it can help to ask a relative or close friend – who doesn't share your powerful attachment to the dog – to assist you with the practical aspects of the process, such as taking you and your dog to the vet, and to support you during the grieving process.

A happy dog will have grown old gracefully, and you will probably have had many enjoyable years with your faithful friend, filled with wonderful memories of good companionship. It is always best to fix your mind on a favourite moment or time with your dog than to dwell on the sadness of the end of your relationship.

Conclusion

The old adage, 'Prevention is better than cure' certainly applies to problems in dogs, whether these are physical or behavioural. Good selective breeding may not completely guarantee fitness but it can help to minimize the incidence of physical (and mental) health problems. However, inoculations against disease, a good healthy diet, regular grooming, and invigorating fresh-air walks will do a great deal to help your German Shepherd Dog stay strong and able enough to fight off most common illnesses. Finally, with good effective training and consistent handling, you can prevent the development of the bad habits and behavioural problems that can cause so much anxiety to owners (as well as to their dogs).

It's good to have a friend that doesn't want to burden you with his problems – that is the truth about unconditional love from dogs – and with a few sensible precautions, a happy, healthy dog will fulfil this role, repaying your care and attention for many years with obedience and faithful companionship.

I sincerely hope that the information offered within this book will benefit you and your dog. Over the years of working in my behaviour clinic I have come into contact with some wonderful dogs and some equally excellent owners. I have learned something important from every German Shepherd case, and I am sure that I shall continue to learn as the years go by. I wish you every success and happiness with your companion German Shepherd Dog. May your dog be free from any physical and mental problems, but, if life should decide to throw any his way, I hope you can both overcome them and that my advice will help make the journey on the road to recovery an easier one to travel.

Index

adopted dog, collecting 71
  handling 76–7
  settling in 72–3
  socializing 73–6
  unknown past of 68–71
  temperament test for 70
  see also re-homing
aggression: classification 81–3
  intraspecific 88–90
  target 86–8
  predatory 90–92
aversion therapy 90

bathing 109–10
breeding 120–3
breed standards 12, 13

car and travel phobias 101–102
castration 32
clicker 49–51
collars 41, 55
commands 45–46, 47
commitment (from owner)
  19–20, 21–2
controlled scenarios 85–90
Control Walk 55–8
coprophagia 97–8
crate 28, 29, 30, 71, 72, 73

diarrhoea 113
diet 31, 72, 110–11
dominance 37, 78, 79, 83–4

environment, creating 28–9,
  72–3
euthanasia 125–6

faulty learning 22
first-aid 117–19

grooming 32, 109–11
guarding instinct 7, 8, 85

hand-signals 47
headcollars see collars
health checks 107–8
hereditary defects 14, 66
house-training 31
human-canine pack 36–7,
  42, 77–9
hyper-attachment see
  Separation-related Disorder

ill health: signs 113, 116
indoor kennel see crate

leadership (owner) 36, 42, 79
lead training 54–5

noise sensitivity 98–101

Obsessive-compulsive
  Disorders (OCDs) 104–6
old age 123–5

parasites 111–12
play 37–40
  rough 39–40
puppy, choosing 25–7
  collecting 27–28
  chewing 31–2
  food and water 31
  initial handling 29
  pre-school for 44

recall, refusal to 92
re-homing 65–8
  reasons for 65–6
rescue centres 67–8

resocialization 73–6
  Introduction Walk 75
retrieval 59–60
reward 44, 46
reward whistle 49, 51–3

search games 60, 62–4
Separation-related Disorder
  (SRD) 92–7
  clinical signs 93
  drug therapy 97
  triggers 95–6
socialization 25, 47–8
  with other pets 33
  with owner 34–6
  see also resocialization
spaying 32
status, communicating 36–7,
  42, 78–9, 83–4, 85
status-seeking 83–4
strays 68
submission 36, 37, 77, 83

toys 38–39
traffic phobias 102–3
training aids 48–54
training discs 49, 53–4
training games 59–64

vet, visits to 32, 119
  phobia 120
visitors 46–7

walks 41–2
  off-lead 58–9
  see also Control Walk;
    Introduction Walk
wolf 9
working GSDs 7–9, 15–17, 66